"I love Mike Gervais—his insights, his straight talk, and his pitch-perfect advice! Mike draws on the latest research and his own practices and principles to explain why we care so much about what other people think of us and what to do about it."

—**ANGELA DUCKWORTH,** bestselling author, *Grit: The Power of Passion and Perseverance*; cofounder, The Character Lab

"Whether our pursuit of being our best is in business, in parenting, or in sports, Michael Gervais's *The First Rule of Mastery* helps us place attention on those elements within our control rather than wasting focus and energy on those that are not."

—**SATYA NADELLA,** CEO, Microsoft

"As a ballet dancer who has dealt with her fair share of criticism, I wholeheartedly recommend *The First Rule of Mastery*. With each page, Michael Gervais gently guides us toward a liberating realization: our worth is not defined by the judgments and opinions of others, but by our own self-awareness, passion, and commitment to our craft."

—**MISTY COPELAND,** principal dancer, American Ballet Theatre

"*The First Rule of Mastery* eloquently and convincingly shares modern insights and timeless wisdom to free us from the fear of other people's opinions (FOPO) so that we can explore our potential, expand our contributions in life, and do so in service of others. The evidence-backed perspective prompts self-reflection and enables action through a practical toolbox for application in the real world."

—**BRADY BREWER,** Executive Vice President, Starbucks Corporation

"It's wild how much we each allow FOPO to shape our days, our confidence, and ultimately the space we take up in the world. This book is an indispensable road map to self-mastery for us all."

—**KERRI WALSH JENNINGS,** five-time Olympian and four-time medalist

"I so wish I had read this book earlier in my life. This is absolutely a game changer for anyone looking to become their very best self—and, most important, their happiest self—in a world that desperately needs us to be both."

—**JULIE FOUDY,** two-time FIFA Women's World Cup champion; two-time Olympic gold medalist

"*The First Rule of Mastery* brilliantly articulates how to navigate the challenges of FOPO. Gervais's insights make it an essential read for leaders seeking to inspire a culture of learning over external validation."

—**KATHLEEN HOGAN,** Chief Human Resources Officer, Microsoft

"*The First Rule of Mastery* brilliantly teaches us to focus on who we genuinely want to be, not on who we imagine others believe we are. This book is a master class on looking inward to determine our own value. Thrilled that this book is available to the world!"

—**APOLO OHNO,** eight-time Olympic medalist

THE FIRST RULE OF MASTERY

THE FIRST RULE OF MASTERY

STOP WORRYING ABOUT WHAT PEOPLE THINK OF YOU

MICHAEL GERVAIS, PhD

WITH KEVIN LAKE

HARVARD BUSINESS REVIEW PRESS

BOSTON, MASSACHUSETTS

Copyright 2024 Michael Gervais

All rights reserved

Printed in the United States of America

10 9 8 7 6 5 4 3 2 1

No part of this publication may be reproduced, stored in or introduced into a retrieval system, or transmitted, in any form, or by any means (electronic, mechanical, photocopying, recording, or otherwise), without the prior permission of the publisher. Requests for permission should be directed to permissions@harvardbusiness.org, or mailed to Permissions, Harvard Business School Publishing, 60 Harvard Way, Boston, Massachusetts 02163.

The web addresses referenced in this book were live and correct at the time of the book's publication but may be subject to change.

Library of Congress Cataloging-in-Publication Data

Names: Gervais, Michael (Psychologist), author. | Lake, Kevin, author.
Title: The first rule of mastery : stop worrying about what people think of you / Michael Gervais (PhD), with Kevin Lake.
Description: Boston, Massachusetts : Harvard Business Review Press, [2023] | Includes index.
Identifiers: LCCN 2023018764 (print) | LCCN 2023018765 (ebook) | ISBN 9781647823245 (hardcover) | ISBN 9781647823252 (epub)
Subjects: LCSH: Success—Psychological aspects. | Performance—Psychological aspects. | Cognitive psychology. | Other (Philosophy)—Psychological aspects. | Fear.
Classification: LCC BF637.S8 G423 2023 (print) | LCC BF637.S8 (ebook) | DDC 158.1—dc23/eng/20230714
LC record available at https://lccn.loc.gov/2023018764
LC ebook record available at https://lccn.loc.gov/2023018765

The paper used in this publication meets the requirements of the American National Standard for Permanence of Paper for Publications and Documents in Libraries and Archives Z39.48-1992.

Contents

Introduction   1

1. Beethoven's Secret   15

PART ONE

Unmask

2. The Mechanics of FOPO   29

3. Fear Factors   45

4. Identity: A Breeding Ground for FOPO   63

5. Outsourcing Self-Worth   87

6. The Neurobiology of FOPO   101

PART TWO

Assess

7. Barry Manilow and the Spotlight Effect   113

8. Do We Really Know What Someone
   Else Is Thinking?   121

9. We See Things as ~~They~~ We Are 137

10. Social Beings Masquerading as Separate Selves 149

PART THREE

Redefine

11. Challenges to Our Closely Held Beliefs 167

12. Look Who's Talking 173

13. The Litmus Test 179

Notes *189*
Index *199*
Acknowledgments *207*
About the Authors *209*

THE FIRST RULE OF MASTERY

Introduction

*Everything that irritates us about others can
lead us to an understanding of ourselves.*

—CARL JUNG

When we give more value to other people's opinions than our
own, we live life on their terms, not ours. Softball star Lauren
Regula grappled with that dilemma in the ramp up to the 2020
Olympics. Having retired from the sport eleven years earlier, Regula was presented with an opportunity of a lifetime—to play
again, for Team Canada, on the sport's biggest stage. To win
an Olympic medal after coming tantalizingly close in 2008
when she came in fourth after a heartbreaking loss in the bronze
medal game in Beijing. The Canadian coach called Regula, a
thirty-nine-year-old mom with three children and a business
with her husband, and tried to lure her out of retirement to take
a final shot at winning an Olympic medal.

In the movie version of this story, Lauren probably screams
with joy. Her reaction serves as an emotional apex—a prime
spot for swells of sentimental strings.

But in the real version, she hesitated.

In her heart, she knew she wanted to do it, but there were
challenges and doubts. Having been to two prior Olympics, she

was also aware she wasn't going to train for a couple of weeks and go home.[1] The pursuit of her dream would mean significant time away from her children, now eleven, ten, and eight years old. Adding to the complexity, the athletes would only be able to leave the quarantine "bubble" one time in the six months leading up to the Games.

"Being a mom, it wasn't an easy decision to say yes to attempting to make an Olympic roster," she told me. "Never mind a mom who had only spent a few months on a field, working at her sport, in the last twelve years. Never mind a mom who owns and runs a business with her hubby."

But ultimately it wasn't age, the extended layoff, or the years she had spent battling postpartum depression that threatened to derail her from Tokyo; it was a gnawing concern for what other people think.

Here's Lauren, in her own words:

> When I shared my story of training, and travel, and my dedication to this dream, these are some of the comments I received:
>
> Oh my gosh, I could never do that. . . . I could never leave my family for that long.
> *(Insert mom judgment.)*
>
> You still think you can do it? I mean, aren't you afraid you'll never be as good as you were?
> *(Insert "Who the hell do you think you are?" judgment.)*

Aren't you, like, the oldest player ever?
(Insert age judgment.)

Is Dave okay with you playing and leaving?
(Insert wife and abandoning my family judgment.)

I stressed about those negative conversations. I stressed about what other people thought about me and my decision. I stressed about other people thinking I was a bad mom and a bad wife. That I was too old. That I'll never be able to do it. And it really made me pause. My world was revolving around what others thought of my decision.

Now, I had more positive opinions than negative; however, I found the negative opinions to be way more magnetic. They held more weight at the time. Being stuck on those negative words, as I see it now, reminds me of one of my favorite quotes. "One tree can make one thousand matches. And one match can burn one thousand trees."

Lauren was wrestling with her assessment of herself against the assessment of her by others. Her dilemma was a challenge we all face in different forms. Do we follow our own internal directives or conform to societal norms and expectations?

To put it another way, Lauren suffered from FOPO—the fear of people's opinions—and it almost cost her one last shot at her dream.

An Invisible Limit

Our fear of people's opinions (FOPO) is a hidden epidemic and may be the single greatest constrictor of human potential.[2] Our concern with what other people think about us has become an irrational, unproductive, and unhealthy obsession in the modern world. And its negative effects reach into all aspects of our lives.

When we experience FOPO, we lose faith in ourselves, and our performance suffers. That's human nature.

But, if we're not careful, FOPO can take over the narrative in our minds, slowly poisoning us. Instead of focusing on our own thoughts and feelings, we start obsessing about the thoughts and opinions of others, whether spoken or perceived, and this obsession can affect our decisions and actions.

And our lives.

Think about Lauren. If she had let her negative thoughts—her fear of people's opinions—take over, she would have missed out on one last chance to do what she'd spent her entire life training to do.

FOPO is part of the human condition because we're operating with an ancient brain. A craving for social approval made our ancestors cautious and savvy thousands of years ago. If the responsibility for the failed hunt fell on your shoulders, your place in the tribe could be threatened.

But today, with the proliferation of social media, the intense pressure to succeed, especially at an early age, and our overreliance on external rewards, metrics, and validation, FOPO is running rampant.

You can see FOPO in action when leaders don't speak up and make tough decisions—or when CEOs privilege short-term shareholder gains over the long-term health of their companies. And when politicians vote with their party instead of their conscience.

The sooner you fundamentally change your relationship with other people's opinions, the sooner you become free. Totally free to be at home with yourself wherever you are.

FOPO shows up almost everywhere in our lives—and the consequences are great. We play it safe and we play it small because we're afraid of what will happen on the other side of the critique. When challenged, we go full-on porcupine, protecting our egos with our version of sharp quills, or we surrender our viewpoint. We trade in authenticity for approval. We don't raise our hand when we can't control the outcome. We try to read the room not out of benevolence, but for belonging. We laugh when it's not funny. We bite our tongue when someone says something offensive. We formulate our response while listening. We pursue power rather than purpose. We please rather than provoke. We chase the dreams of others rather than our own.

We externalize our self-esteem, our sense of value. We see ourselves through the eyes of others. We look outside of ourselves to determine how we feel about ourselves.

If people approve of us, or the choices we make, we feel great. If others disapprove of us or the choices we make, we feel terrible.

We scamper around the world trying to please others and being who we think people want us to be, rather than who we are. We are unaware of our own needs or we dismiss our needs as we hustle for our self-worth.

We will have spent our brief time on this incredible planet playing a role, inhabiting an identity, conforming to the perceived expectations of others. We will never discover who we are truly capable of becoming.

Now, think about decisions you've made in your life. Did you choose your career path because you were passionate about the field, or did you pursue law or business or whatever because that's what you were supposed to do? Or, let me put it this way: Have you ever felt the urge to make a change in your life, or boldly step into a new challenge, but didn't because of what other people might think?

We all have.

But here's the thing: if you start paying less and less attention to what makes you *you*—your talents, beliefs, and values—and start conforming to what others may or *may not* think, you'll dramatically limit your potential and your pursuit of mastery.

We all have unique qualities and strengths—and it's our job to make the most of them. We're always in a state of becoming— and that state, that striving for becoming the person we want to be, is tenuous and easily lost amid the internal and external pressures of daily life. It takes deep inner resolve and vision to pull off.[3]

If you're overly influenced by outside forces, such as other people's opinions or societal pressures, they can box you in and limit what's possible.[4] Instead of making the next move, you may tell yourself, *The odds are against me or I'm not smart enough.* Instead of making a career change, you may say, *I'm too old.* If left unexamined, these stories can feel real, true, and immutable.

The desire to fit in and the paralyzing fear of being disliked undermine our ability to pursue the lives we want to create.

Though our ancient brains make FOPO an everyday reality, that doesn't mean that we need to obsess over it—to prevent us from doing what we want to do.

Space in Between

Woody Hoburg's story underscores the possibility that opens up when we follow our own path and don't succumb to the opinions of others. Woody is one of the best humans I've ever met. He fires on all cylinders—emotionally, psychologically, intellectually, and physically. His sense of adventure is matched only by his curiosity and humility. Since he was a kid, he loved to climb and he dreamed of going to space. Woody earned a bachelor's degree in aeronautics and astronautics from MIT and went on to Berkeley to pursue his doctorate in computer science.

Woody loved solving technical, hard problems but he had another side of him that didn't feel captured on that path. At Berkeley, he was climbing on the weekends in nearby Yosemite, and he was flying planes, but he wanted his adventures to be more structured and meaningful. He wanted to put his skills to work in a job that was purposeful. He came up with the idea of getting his EMT certification and applying to the Yosemite Search and Rescue team.

Performing mountain rescues is completely unrelated to pursuing a PhD in computer science, so Woody sought the counsel of his academic mentors, people he deeply respected and still considers friends and mentors to this day. He was fascinated by how many of them tried to discourage him, telling him things like "I don't think it's such a good idea. I'm not sure how that's going to help you in what you are pursuing."

The opinions of academics carry weight when you are on the academia track. As described by Woody, "These are people I deeply trust and respect, and I wanted to listen to their opinions." But Woody resisted the temptation to conform. "At the end of the day, I just had to make a choice. . . . I just knew I was going to do it and I'm so glad I did because it was one of the best experiences of my life."

Woody finished his PhD at Berkeley, started teaching at MIT, and was training in a climbing gym when his best friend told him NASA was accepting applications for astronauts after a four-year hiatus. Woody filled out an internet form at USAjobs.gov and pressed submit with what he deemed to be a "zero probability" of getting in. A year and a half later, he was one of twelve candidates selected for the astronaut class from more than eighteen thousand qualified applicants. At the time of this writing, Dr. Hoburg is at the International Space Station at the front end of a six-month mission. He and I just finished recording the first-ever podcast from outer space.

Why did Woody get selected? He believes joining Yosemite Search and Rescue distinguished his candidacy. His refusal to bow to the pressure of other people's opinions punched his ticket to space and allowed him to realize his childhood dream.

In the Trenches

As a high-performance psychologist, I've had the privilege of working with some of the most extraordinary individuals and teams across the planet. I was on the sidelines when the Seattle

Seahawks won Super Bowl XLVIII against the Denver Broncos. I sat in mission control when Austrian base jumper Felix Baumgartner made his record-breaking space jump from twenty-four miles above the earth's surface, free-falling at over eight hundred miles per hour. I was on the beaches of Tokyo when USA Surfing won the first Olympic gold medal in the history of the sport. I was courtside when Kerri Walsh Jennings and Misty May-Treanor, arguably the best female beach volleyball team of all time, won three golds in three consecutive Olympics. I was in the room with the CEO of the world's largest tech company when the company set course to be the first enterprise organization to build a culture based on mindset, empathy, and purpose.

The best performers in the world push past the perceived limits of human potential and expand our notions of what's possible.

But, in my experience, they aren't merely exceptional at their craft. Beyond a relentless pursuit of being their best, what drives these high performers is a striving for inner excellence. They're in constant pursuit of mastery.

And it's not easy. Though we tend to look at athletes, actors, leaders, and musicians as superhumans who possess innate physical skills and mental toughness, reality is much more complicated.

In fact, success—especially when achieved in the public eye—makes us more susceptible to FOPO.

Imagine being subjected to a 24-7 feedback loop of criticism—and praise—from fans, media, and social media users. If you're a pop star or an actress, imagine having to constantly read comments and reviews about your voice, your looks, and your abilities. Wouldn't that gnaw at you, too?

Or imagine dedicating your entire life to making it to the pinnacle of your sport and realizing that the allure of power and fame can be a trap that leads to loneliness and depression.

Or imagine if your success in life was measured by a simple metric: wins. This can be especially hard for Olympians who train their entire lives for a single event, which, in some cases, lasts less than a minute. Imagine finishing in fourth place—a blink of an eye away from medaling.

We see this in corporate life, too. The higher you rise on the career ladder, the more susceptible you are to scrutiny and public opinion. Leaders have the power to make decisions that significantly impact stakeholders—employees, customers, shareholders, and the general public—and their actions and decisions are more likely to attract attention and opinions from these groups. Media coverage further amplifies public opinions and puts additional pressure on leaders to manage their public image effectively. Which is why leadership is rife with FOPO.

My point is that focusing on externals—things that are beyond our control—is all too common and doesn't magically go away with success.

That's why it's important to begin the process and mental work of changing our focus to what we can control—ourselves.

Mastery in any area of life—the arts, business, parenting, sports—requires being able to differentiate what is and is not within our control.

When we place attention on things outside our control, we take our focus and energy away from what we can control.

Hence, the first rule of mastery requires looking within and fundamentally committing to work on mastering what's 100 percent under your control. There is nothing else that can be mastered. This is the essence of the path.

Leaning In to FOPO

In high-performing sports, athletes frontload awareness and psychological skill building, so that when they are faced with a challenge they have internal tools to successfully navigate the experience. That same approach applies to transforming our relationship with the perceived opinions and judgments of others.

The ambition of this book is to illuminate a psychological process that lives just beneath the surface and turn it into your best teacher. Use FOPO as an opportunity. Start to identify it in your life. Use your reactions as a springboard to a better understanding of yourself. Recognize how you are choosing to think and behave in response to the perceived judgments of others.

Each chapter provides an insight or lesson in how to use FOPO to unlock your potential.

Rather than running away from or ignoring FOPO, choose to see it as a learning opportunity, a potential stepping stone to unlocking your potential. Use it to discover aspects of yourself that have remained hidden. When FOPO surfaces, lean in to discover what's underneath the fear.

For example, you have a great idea in the client meeting, but you don't raise your hand. Investigate what that's about. Do you want the idea to be fully worked out before you dare share it? Are you afraid you won't be able to eloquently express yourself? Are you concerned that your idea won't be received well? If the latter, what if people didn't embrace your idea? Does that mean you are not competent? Or that you are not good enough? Keep pulling on that thread to discover what's at the root of your fear. What is the story you are telling yourself?

Developing an awareness of our fears about the opinions of others is the first step to discharging the power they hold over us. Awareness as the starting point for change is not a novel idea. Every self-development book, every New Year's Eve resolution, every twelve-step program is anchored in awareness. We cannot even contemplate change unless we are aware of the challenge we want to address.

But awareness is only the first step. Awareness must be accompanied by psychological skill building. Someone could be having a panic attack and be acutely aware that their thoughts are driving it but lack the skills to work with those thoughts.

Lauren is a prime example. She did not allow FOPO to dictate the course of her life. A year delayed because of the pandemic, she went to Tokyo with Team Canada in 2021 and, at age thirty-nine, found herself standing on the Olympic podium holding a bronze medal.

Lauren, though, did not forget that her dream could have easily been derailed:

FOPO. It's real.

And I almost let it get in my way.

Thank goodness I didn't.

Thank goodness I had the confidence to listen to me.

So ask yourself . . .

Is FOPO holding you back?[5]

1

Beethoven's Secret

*An artist must never be a prisoner
of himself, prisoner of a style, prisoner of
a reputation, prisoner of success.*

—HENRI MATISSE

No one is immune to FOPO—not you, not me, not world-class athletes. Even renowned artists, such as one of the greatest and most prolific composers ever, get waylaid by FOPO's power.

But only after we confront FOPO's forces can we truly set forth on the path to mastery.

Consider Beethoven.

To many people, he seemed like a vessel handpicked by God to channel music from a higher plane. His work transformed every genre of classical music. He broke all the rules to create some of the most transcendent music the world has ever known. He embodied the idea of the creative genius who railed against convention and forged his own artistic path.

Despite being one of the most fearless artists to ever walk the planet, Beethoven lived for three years in abject fear of others' opinions.

Near the apex of his career, Beethoven receded from public view. He carried a secret that he thought, if revealed, would destroy his professional life. The archetypal creative artist seemingly born to struggle against fate and the injustices of the world chose to socially isolate rather than utter three words aloud.

"I am deaf."

Beethoven started losing his hearing in his mid-twenties. The cruel irony of losing the sense most relevant to his art and livelihood drove him on a futile search for cures, ranging from almond oil earplugs to baths to toxic tree bark. During those early years, he did not talk about his deteriorating hearing to anyone outside the medical community. As he was increasingly externally celebrated in society, he was trapped alone inside a world with his own distressing thoughts and feelings.

To conceal his hearing loss, he masqueraded behind the trope of the genius artist whose brain was preoccupied with other intellectual activity. When he couldn't hear what someone said or a sound they referenced, the other person would assume (with Beethoven's influence) that it was a function of inattention or forgetfulness: "It is surprising that some people have never noticed my deafness; but since I have always been liable to fits of absentmindedness, they attribute my hardness of hearing to that. Sometimes too I can scarcely hear a person who speaks softly; I can hear sounds, it is true, but cannot make out the words. But if anyone shouts, I can't bear it. Heaven alone knows what is to become of me."[1]

Beethoven was deeply concerned about the impact his hearing loss would have on his music, especially his ability to play the piano, but public perception presented an equally powerful threat. "If I belonged to any other profession it would be easier, but in my profession it is an awful state, the more since my enemies, who are not few, what would they say?"[2] He feared that his detractors would use the revelation against him. He was worried their criticism would lead to discrimination against him and exclusion from the Viennese music circles that he had toiled for so long to access. Beethoven, like other artists of the times, was dependent on aristocratic patronage. Overcoming the stigma might be a taller hill to climb than the loss of hearing itself.

But the greatest threat of all may have been to Beethoven's identity. "Ah how could I possibly admit such an infirmity in the one sense which should have been more perfect in me than in others, a sense which I once possessed in highest perfection, a perfection such as few surely in my profession enjoy or have enjoyed," he wrote to his brother.[3]

He was Beethoven the music god, and music gods were supposed to hear music better than mortals. His auditory loss did not fit with the idea he held of himself or the public image he promoted. He had a rigid identity—conditioned upon approval and praise from others—that was as real and immutable to him as his skin and bones. As reflected in a letter to his generous benefactor, Prince Lichnowsky, his identity bordered on myth-making: "Prince! What you are, you are by circumstance and by birth. What I am, I am through myself. Of princes there have been and will be thousands. Of Beethovens there is only one."[4]

Beethoven responded how most of us respond when we feel our survival is threatened. He tried to protect himself. Rather than looking inward and altering the way he saw himself, he looked outward and tried to conform external reality to his perception of himself.

Beethoven paid an exorbitant price to architect a reality that kept the opinions of other people at bay. He often couldn't hear people talk but was afraid to ask them to speak louder for fear of being found out.

He played the role of misanthrope to keep his secret hidden. He spent several years isolated from society, alone in his deafness, even contemplating suicide.

Daddy Problems

From a young age Beethoven had been conditioned to believe external opinions mattered. His father, Johann, a mediocre tenor whose own music aspirations were thwarted by alcoholism, sought to live out his dreams through his son. He appointed himself as Beethoven's instructor and verbally and physically abused Beethoven to push him harder. He kept him in line with shouts, threats, and beatings, even locking him in the basement.[5] On one occasion after returning from a night out with friends, Johann made little Beethoven stand on a stool to reach the piano keys and perform for his friends, beating him whenever he missed a note.

As the young Beethoven's talents became more apparent, Johann set his sights on his becoming Europe's next music sensation. Johann played the role of eighteenth-century stage dad, a marketeer who promoted Beethoven across all the music circles in Bonn, Germany. When Beethoven was seven, his father lied about his age by a year to more closely fit the archetype of prodigy. He rented a hall in Cologne and took out an ad in the local newspaper, advertising his "little son of six years" who had already had the honor of playing for the Court.[6] From a young age, Beethoven was given the not-so-subtle message, "You are not enough as you are."

Early on, Beethoven recognized that his upward movement through the music world of nineteenth-century Vienna would be directly correlated to the status and opinions of those who admired him. On a deeper level, he had firsthand experience that approval and love came in response to performance and achievement. His father's actions sent a clear message that Beethoven was loved not for who he was but for what he did. The fusion of love and approval often creates a pattern of approval seeking in later life—and the spotlight fueled Beethoven's sense of self.

Sanctuary

Beethoven had one place he could go that was impenetrable to the opinions of others, inhospitable to self-doubt, and beyond the reach of the aristocratic patrons who provided the financial lifeline for his music—his inner world.

Beethoven developed the ability to fully immerse himself in his music and disappear inside himself, oblivious to his surroundings and without any sense of self-consciousness. He could be anywhere—scribbling in his notebooks or improvising amid a great crowd.

A childhood friend recalled one of those moments. She was talking to Beethoven, but he seemed to be absent, unable to hear her. When he finally snapped back, he responded, "Oh, please, no, no, forgive me! I was busy with such a beautiful, deep thought I couldn't bear to be disturbed."[7] Biographer Jan Swafford described it as a "trance" where "he found solitude even in company."[8] A family friend who was instrumental in shaping Beethoven's early career gave the state of mind a name, "raptus."[9] Beethoven's raptus became a legend among those in Beethoven's inner circle. When he would withdraw, it wouldn't be uncommon to hear "He has his raptus again today."[10]

With his raptus, Beethoven developed an internal skill set that allowed him to focus on his music and block out internal and external distractions. He was able to go to a place where the opinions of others did not matter. He was comfortable venturing inside his own cave because he knew how to be with himself. He knew how to listen to his own music.

The challenge was when he emerged from raptus and was back in the approval game.

Facing FOPO

Beethoven reached a point where it was getting impossible to conceal his deafness. He described his bind in a heartfelt and anguished letter he wrote to his brothers on October 6, 1802, known as the Heiligenstadt Testament.[11]

> Oh you men who think or say that I am malevolent, stubborn, or misanthropic, how greatly do you wrong me. You do not know the secret cause which makes me

seem that way to you. . . . forgive me when you see me
draw back when I would gladly mingle with you: . . .
I must live like an exile, if I approach near to people a
hot terror seizes upon me, a fear that I may be subjected
to the danger of letting my condition be observed. . . .
what a humiliation for me when someone standing next
to me heard a flute in the distance and I heard nothing,
or someone standing next to me heard a shepherd
singing and again I heard nothing. Such incidents drove
me almost to despair; a little more of that and I would
have ended my life.

The romantic version of change is that we observe a shift in
our physical, psychological, or environmental conditions and
we recognize we need to make a change. We confront the challenge. We take the risk, make the change, and then reap the
rewards of it.

Unfortunately, that's more the exception than the rule.
Deeply rooted patterns and behaviors make change difficult.
We know we should change, but we often don't make a change
until we have to. We hit rock bottom. Or the pain becomes
intolerable. We are forced to reexamine how we are working
in the world.

In my experience, pain is often what makes us change. That
certainly was the case with Beethoven.

The Heiligenstadt Testament is Beethoven at rock bottom,
but it also marked a fundamental shift in Beethoven's relationship with social approval and acceptance and, not coincidentally,
opened the floodgates for one of the greatest creative outpour-
ings in human history. After spelling out his despair, Beethoven

accepted his deafness as a part of himself and resolved to fully develop his artistic capacities regardless of the cost: "I would have put an end to my life—only art it was that withheld me, ah it seemed impossible to leave the world until I had produced all that I felt called upon me to produce. . . . Patience, they say, is what I must now choose for my guide, and I have done so."

Beethoven decided to expose his greatest fear, and in doing so he freed himself from the paralyzing grip of FOPO. "All evil is mysterious and appears greatest when viewed in solitude," he wrote. "Discussed with others it seems more endurable because one becomes entirely familiar with that which we dread, feeling as if it has been overcome."[12] Rather than destroying his life, the admission freed him in ways that were unimaginable. No longer trying to manage other people's perceptions of him, he regained control of his life.

The Path of Mastery

When Beethoven stopped worrying about what other people thought about him, he shifted from performing for the world outside of him to performing from the world inside him. When he embraced the first rule, he crossed over to the path to mastery.

Mastery is an inner-directed life externally expressed. With no finish line to cross, mastery is a love affair with experience, honesty, truth, and continual exploration. One cannot step on to the path of mastery until making a fundamental commitment to work from the inside out.

Technical excellence alone is not sufficient to travel the path to mastery. If you are not creating from a place in alignment with who you are, you are just a great performer, not a master. If your orientation is to take the temperature of the world around you before tapping into the fire inside you, you will never unlock your potential.

Mastery is not comparative. If the pre–Heiligenstadt Testament Beethoven had been held up against the great composers who preceded him, the consensus likely would have been that he was a master. But measuring Beethoven's mastery against Bach's or Mozart's is meaningless.

The foundational measuring stick for mastery is what each of us, individually, is capable of becoming—and we don't know what that looks like until we embrace the first rule of mastery.

The More We Value Things outside Our Control, the Less Control We Have

Beethoven stopped squandering his internal resources trying to influence conditions he did not have complete control over and mastered what was within his control.

He gave up his career as a virtuoso pianist to concentrate on composing. When Beethoven let go of who he thought he was supposed to be, he became who he was fully capable of becoming. He created a world of sound different from anything heard before.

Near the end of his life, the deaf Beethoven wrote his final symphony, one of the greatest accomplishments in the history of music. In his first onstage performance in more than a decade, Beethoven "conducted" the orchestra at the premiere of the Ninth Symphony at Vienna's Theater am Kärntnertor on May 7, 1824. Due to his deafness, the musicians had been instructed to follow the actual conductor, Michael Umhauf. But Beethoven couldn't resist showing the musicians the style and energy he wanted in the piece, animatedly throwing himself into the music for an orchestra that for him was soundless.[13] At the end of the performance, Beethoven remained facing the orchestra and could not hear the audience behind him. The contralto gently tapped Beethoven and turned him toward the crowd to witness their thunderous applause and the sea of waving handkerchiefs and hats held up in the air.

We often try to control other people's opinions and how they think about us, but ironically, in the desire for approval we give up control of our own lives. As Lao Tzu, the philosopher and reputed author of the Tao Te Ching, and the founder of Taoism said, "Care about what other people think and you will always be their prisoner."

From Idea to Action

Let's do an exercise so we are clear about the things we actually control. You can visualize what I'm saying or you can pull out a pen and paper and write it down (see figure 1-1).

Draw a big circle and a smaller inner circle inside, so it almost looks like a donut. In the outer circle list all the things that matter in life but that you don't have 100 percent control over. Start with other people's opinions, since it's pretty clear we don't have control over those. Add things like

FIGURE 1-1

What's in your control—and what's not

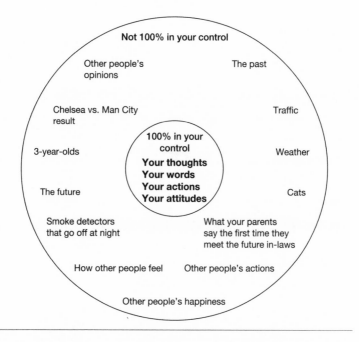

weather. The sports teams you care about. Bosses. Market conditions. Workplace environment. It's a long list.

In the smaller circle, list those things that are 100 percent under your control—things like the time you arrive at work. How you communicate with your children. Your effort on the playing field.

So, what is your capacity to control 100 percent of the time? What's not in your control?

PART ONE

UNMASK

2

The Mechanics of FOPO

Opinion is ultimately determined by the
feelings, and not by the intellect.

—HERBERT SPENCER

I had a conversation with Moby, the visionary, Grammy Award–winning music artist where he described the intoxication of being on the receiving end of external validation:

I saw myself on the cover of a magazine in early days as a musician and I was like, "Oh my God, this is validation. This is love. People know me. That means I have meaning. They care about me. They're being nice to me. I have friends I've never met." And so I spent the next fifteen years obsessing over what people said about me because for a minute, it was really good. I mean it sounds like I'm also describing alcohol and drugs. Like in the beginning, "How great is this? . . . the answer to all my problems." And then slowly, over time, you realize it's destroying you.[1]

Moby is a bit of a philosopher-musician and the passage of time gave him a clear view of the dynamics of the opinion game. Rather than continuing to react to the world outside him, Moby made a shift:

> I've been living in the public eye for quite a long time now, and I don't pay attention to how anyone might want to label me. I stopped reading social media comments. I stopped reading reviews. I stopped watching interviews of myself a long time ago because the simple illogic of it finally struck me. I hope that maybe this is helpful to anyone who's listening: think of how strange it is that we hand our sense of self—that we hand our emotional state—over to strangers, over to people we've never met and people who might just be bots on Macedonian troll farms. . . . I realized a while ago that I cannot stay sane and calm if I'm constantly being torn apart by the opinions of people I've never actually met.

Moby unplugged from the opinions of people he did not know and who did not know him. "I cannot take it personally because they're not responding to a person. They're responding to a photo or an image or an idea."

As Moby recognized, there's a space, or gap, in between any given stimulus and our response.[2] One of the great privileges of being human is that, within that space, we have the freedom and power to choose how we respond. While we may not have control over the events that occur in our lives, we do have control over our reactions and attitudes toward them. By consciously choosing our response, we can break free from automatic patterns, habits, and conditioned behaviors.

Initially, Moby felt like his experience was "something that was only germane to public figures" like "professional athletes or actors or musicians or politicians, but now it is literally everyone with a phone and a social media account." As he described it, "Everyone's a public figure. The guy who works at my local supermarket, putting stuff in the bag, he's a public figure because he has an Instagram account. He might have twenty followers (but) that's public."

Turning to public opinion to see if we are okay, or to measure our social value, is an increasingly common phenomenon in the digital age, but the masses can be a really dangerous tuning fork.

An Internal Gauge

We are inherently inclined to form and maintain relations with other people. Sociability is a characteristic found in all cultures and is a defining aspect of what it means to be human. From an evolutionary perspective, humans have always lived in groups to protect against predators and gain access to resources. But our social natures are driven by more than just pragmatic survival needs. We have a natural desire for connection and belonging that is critical to our mental and emotional health. We have a foundational need to feel loved, accepted, and valued by others, and we often seek out relationships that elicit these feelings.

And given that our survival and reproduction are essentially dependent on our social relationships, we need to be able to assess if and how we fit into the social fabric.

Duke psychologist and neuroscientist Dr. Mark Leary may have identified that mechanism. While doing research about rejection, Leary found that people's self-esteem rises when they feel accepted and plummets when they feel rejected. But that finding didn't make sense to Leary, because self-esteem was widely considered to be a private self-evaluation of one's general sense of happiness with who they are. In theory, our self-esteem should be independent from how other people treat us.

Leary took a deep dive to understand why we are wired that way. Why is our self-esteem so sensitive to acceptance or rejection? His decades-long research upended the commonly held perspective of self-esteem. Rather than reflecting our own regard for ourselves, self-esteem, in Leary's view, provides "ongoing feedback about where we stand in the eyes of others."[3] Leary posits that it's an internal gauge, or meter, that lets us know, in real time, how we are regarded by others.

From an evolutionary perspective, self-esteem has developed as a monitoring mechanism for the quality of our relationships. The system monitors other people's reactions to our behaviors and sends an alarm that alerts us to any possible changes in our inclusion status. The monitoring system generally operates nonconsciously until it detects that our relational value is falling or low. When the alarm bell rings, the threat to our social bonds is pushed into conscious awareness and we evaluate the situation. *Am I being accepted or am I being pushed out? Do I need to adjust my behaviors to fix the relationship?*

With such a high value for survival enmeshed with relationships, it makes sense that the way we mobilize our internal resources around relationships would be highly networked in our brain and body. It also makes sense that we would develop specific mechanisms to attend to minimizing rejection and enhancing acceptance. The continuous scanning is normal, a part of being human. We all have an interpersonal process of searching for cues from the environment to assess our value in the social structure.

What makes less sense is FOPO.

If Leary's sociometer is the healthy gauge by which we attune to our social relationships, FOPO is its maladaptive shadow self.

Rather than calibrating the feedback we are getting from other people against our own sense of self, we allow other people to determine our value. With FOPO, we reflexively overvalue the opinion of others. We dangerously defer the value we hold in a relationship to the other person. In allowing others to assign a value to us, we find ourselves, on a biological level, continuously preoccupied with our own survival.

Defining Characteristics of FOPO

FOPO is an *anticipatory* mechanism that involves psychological, physiological, and physical activation to avoiding rejection and fostering interpersonal connection. It is a preemptive process to increase relational acceptance and avoid rejection. Instead of *Oh, I'd better course-correct based on real feedback about an event and my own internal perspective*, FOPO attempts to look around corners: *Oh, I'd better course-correct before*

I receive any confirming data based on what I imagine could happen.

FOPO is also characterized by a hypervigilant social readiness, relentlessly checking and scanning in search of approval. Overvaluing what others *might* be thinking, we become highly attuned to signals of potential rejection.

FOPO is an exhaustive attempt to interpret what others are thinking in an effort to avoid negative evaluation by them. It is not the actual negative opinion that is so problematic; it's a fear of that opinion. We attempt to preempt a negative opinion by persistently interpreting clues in our environment. We visually read body language, microexpressions, words, silence, actions, and inactions.

FOPO is interpersonal dependent but it's an intrapersonal experience. It is a thought, feeling, or perception that takes place within an individual (intradependent), but the experience is driven by the individual's concerns about how they are perceived by others or how their actions or choices will be received by others (interdependent).

FOPO is a latent filter for decision-making, informing how we think, speak, and act. It can lead people to make choices or take actions that they believe will be more socially acceptable or less likely to be criticized by others, rather than making choices based on their own personal values or preferences.

FOPO is a nonclinical pattern to avoid unfavorable opinions of others. Though FOPO does not meet the criteria of clinical diagnosis, it creates significant distress.

Like applications that quietly run in the background of a computer and consume memory, processing power, and battery life, and ultimately slow down the performance, FOPO burns a lot of our internal resources. Controlling the narrative, managing the perception of others, suppressing our own opinions, being overly apologetic, agreeing with others to avoid appearing disagreeable, going to great lengths to please, the self-deprecating humor to play down our strengths and positive traits, contorting and conforming, overcompensating for perceived shortcomings, seeking validation, the increased heart rate, the muscle tension, the nervousness: FOPO exhausts our system.

FOPO Loop

Imagine you're in a one-on-one with your boss or pitching an important client or on a first date. If you catch a bad case of FOPO—and we've all been there—you probably won't be able to listen intently and live in the flow of the conversation.

Why? Because FOPO evokes a circular psychological and behavioral cycle that is categorized by a set of conditions that occur before (anticipation), during (checking), and after an interpersonal engagement (responding) (see figure 2-1).

Anticipation Phase

In the anticipation phase, individuals experiencing FOPO become preoccupied with playing out scenarios to gauge the likelihood of acceptance or rejection from others. They frequently ask themselves questions such as *Will I be accepted if . . . ?* or *What will they think of me if . . . ?* People use their imagination to entertain how they are going to be perceived and accepted by others. They are less focused on the experience and instead

FIGURE 2-1

FOPO phases

FOPO evokes a circular psychological and behavioral cycle that can be categorized by a set of conditions that take place: a) before an event, b) during an event, and c) after an event.

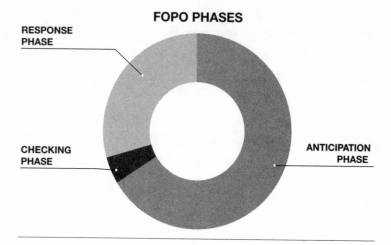

FOPO PHASES

RESPONSE PHASE

CHECKING PHASE

ANTICIPATION PHASE

perseverate on how the other person may or may not feel about them. In that interaction, the problem they are trying to solve is approval or rejection as opposed to the shared social experience.

While it is natural for people to want to be valued and accepted by others—the approval of our supervisors is impactful to our careers—the preoccupation with the perceived opinions of others can undermine meaningful interactions. As a consequence, our excitement, curiosity, and openness to new ideas are squashed.

In a business meeting, we can be so focused on our own acceptance or rejection that we lose our ability to fully consider the potential benefits and drawbacks of the ideas being presented and how they align with the team's overall mission.

In a romantic relationship, we may be so preoccupied with whether our partner will accept or reject us that we fail to fully appreciate and enjoy the shared experiences and connection we have with that person.

Understanding and valuing other people's opinions is a component of social intelligence, but it's problematic when the perceived opinions of others become the prime driver of our thoughts and actions.

Rather than using our imagination for creative, productive, or fulfilling ends, it's directed toward something 100 percent outside our control.

The attentional cost of the anticipatory phase of FOPO is significant. To be great at anything in life, we need to drive attention to the present moment.

The persistent rumination of FOPO pulls resources away from being able to sustain deep focus on the task at hand (required for growth and improvement), inhibits our ability to take in new information and ideas, and creates a tax on human energy, which in return necessitates even greater recovery.

Checking Phase

During the checking phase, which occurs during the actual interaction, individuals relentlessly scan for external cues of acceptance or rejection. These cues include microexpressions, tone of voice, body language, and nonverbal cues. This constant monitoring can be exhausting and can prevent individuals from fully engaging in the interaction and enjoying the experience.

Microexpressions are brief, involuntary facial expressions that can reveal a person's feelings toward us. They are most commonly seen in the eyes, mouth, and forehead. The wrinkled nose and raised upper lip might indicate disgust or contempt, whereas a thin smile signals acceptance.

Tone of voice can provide a clue to relational standing. For example, a monotone expression could suggest a lack of interest, while an animated tone hints at enthusiasm and a desire to engage. A soft, soothing tone might signal empathy and compassion, while a harsh or critical tone may be a telltale sign the other person is displeased with us. Volume, pace. and inflection can also give insight into the other person's feelings and attitudes about us.

Body language provides a window into the unspoken opinions of another. Direct eye contact can indicate interest or engagement, while glancing away can be a sign of discomfort or lack of interest. Open posture—uncrossed arms and legs—suggests approachability and openness, whereas crossed arms and legs denote defensiveness. Nodding suggests agreement while leaning away hints at a lack of interest.

Lastly, word choice can give us a clue as to where we stand in the eyes of another. Inclusive language like "we" or "us" connotes acceptance or being part of a team, while "they" or "them" is other-centered and hints at exclusion. Using your name can indicate you are being seen and acknowledged while calling you "Dave" when your name is Mike can be a harbinger that you are not highly valued.

Much like the anticipation phase, there's a high attentional cost to scanning for cues during the checking phase. If you are hyperfocused on someone's microexpressions, voice, body language, and words for clues as to how they feel about you, there's a good chance you will miss important aspects of the interaction, which limits possibilities for deeper engagement and connection. The unhealthy search for cues and clues also gets in the way of contributing your full knowledge, skills, and ideas and constrains your ability to effectively communicate. It's like rubbernecking as you pass a crash site on the highway.

Yes, you can both see the crash site and drive forward but technically you can only attend to one thing at a time. You are either looking at the crash site or you are looking where you want to go. Attention is a zero-sum game. The time you spend checking is time diverted away from the actual experience.

How we read and interpret those cues is not an exact science. At best, it's an inexact science built on moods, early childhood experiences, untrained mental frameworks, cognitive biases, and cultural differences. And, as we'll see later, our abilities to read these cues aren't so great. We're often wrong.

So we waste a lot of time and resources devoted to something we're not very good at to begin with.

Responding Phase

The last phase is how we react after we take in the perceived cues. *"Am I good" with the other person? Do I feel accepted?* If the answer is "yes," the FOPO cycle ends until there's a new stimulus. Temporary relief is at hand. If the answer is "no," or "I'm not sure," a person with FOPO responds in one of five ways.

You contort to fit in. You sacrifice authentic expression on the altar of approval. You twist yourself into a shape that appears socially acceptable but it's performative in nature. The response does not represent your authentic self. Contorting creates a temporary relief but leaves you feeling disconnected from others. Because you don't share your true self, you never feel connected, understood, or embraced, nor do you become a trusted member of the community. By pretending to be someone you're not, you constantly feel the pressure to maintain the facade. This can intensify the feelings of insecurity and fear of exposure.

The second common response is to conform to the perceived social norms. We align our behavior and attitudes with those of the individual, group, or society. This can lead to a sense of belonging and acceptance, but limits our ability to think and act independently. We avoid expressing contrary opinions. We feign liking or disliking a movie, a song, or an activity to mirror the prevailing view of an individual or group. We go along with an action or decision even if we personally disagree with it. We pretend to have the same beliefs or political views. Conforming to social norms can lead to anxiety, depression, and other mental health issues.

Confrontation is a third response. We may initiate conflict to see how others react so we can gauge whether we are accepted or rejected by a person or group. If we get a lot of attention, we might use that as an indicator that we matter to the other person(s). If we get critiqued, we might go on the attack.

A confrontational approach can also be subtle. For example, someone makes a self-deprecating comment about not being well-liked, and then brushes it off as a joke when they receive positive feedback. It's a way to confront the fear of rejection while also avoiding the vulnerability of expressing a genuine desire for acceptance.

Disconnecting from the relationship is another way we respond to potential social rejection. We might end a romantic relationship, cut ties with friends or family members, or leave our job rather than stay in the ambiguity of not knowing if actual rejection is taking place.

The last and healthiest response to potential rejection is to turn inward and respond based on our own internal standards.

In this scenario, we use FOPO as a cue to invest in more self-discovery, to build psychological skills, and maybe even read a book about FOPO. The goal, each and every time you hear the chimes of FOPO, is to focus more on who you want to be, versus who you think they want you to be.

On-Ramps to FOPO

As you pay more attention, you're likely to discover that certain things accelerate FOPO. Though we're all different, I've found that there are two common on-ramps (see figure 2-2).

A poor sense of self is the most common on-ramp to FOPO. When we lack a clear, stable, and positive understanding of who we are, we often look outside ourselves to see how we feel about ourselves.

We assume others can see us better than we can see ourselves and, as a result, we give power and credibility to other people's

FIGURE 2-2

On-ramps to FOPO

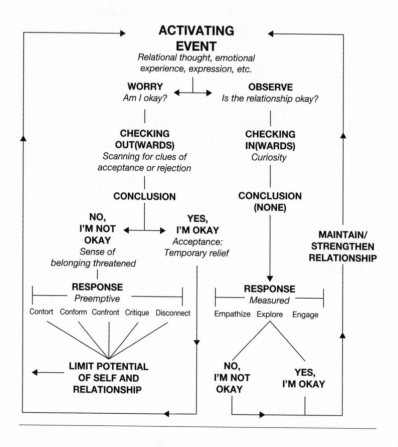

opinions. We rely on the other person to provide signals of approval or potential rejection.

A performance-based identity is also a fast track to FOPO. Performance-based identity, which we discuss in chapter 4, is when one's identity is defined by our performance. We define ourselves by how well we perform in relationship to others. We condition ourselves to look outward for self-definition and, in the process, learn to value external feedback more highly than our own internal feedback.

From Idea to Action

To gain a deeper understanding of your relationship with the three phases of the FOPO loop, you can purposefully create an uncomfortable condition and observe your responses throughout each phase. Here's a simple example.

Begin by browsing through your closet and intentionally select a few clothing items that don't fit or are significantly outdated. Choose something that genuinely makes you feel unattractive, uncomfortable, and uncool.

Next, pair that outfit with a social activity that amplifies your discomfort. It could be a work event, a social gathering, or even a solo activity like having lunch alone in a crowded place.

The exercise commences when you start getting dressed. Take note of your mental activity and observe how you anticipate an impending socially awkward situation. Pay attention to the thoughts that arise. Do you internally rationalize why you shouldn't go through with the exercise? Or do you feel curious about the experience and wonder how it will unfold when you encounter someone? Pay attention to what you say to yourself about yourself. Continue to be mindful and observant of your internal experience, without judgment, until you arrive at the social setting.

Once you arrive, explore your "checking" process and observe how you assess your own well-being (if you engage in such checking at all). Take note of any internal activity that occurs, apart from being fully present and engaged in the social activity.

The third phase of your experiment involves becoming more aware of your response tendencies. Do you feel inclined to do something special to gain acceptance, such as smiling excessively or being overly agreeable? Do you become agitated when it appears the other person is less accepting or uninterested in engaging with you? Alternatively, do you find a sense of peace and freedom?

Embrace the opportunity to have fun with this exercise. Approach it with a playful and exploratory mindset. By doing so, you can uncover valuable insights about yourself and your relationship with FOPO.

3

Fear Factors

*Courage is not the absence of fear, but the triumph
over it. The brave man is not he who does not
feel afraid, but he who conquers that fear.*

—NELSON MANDELA

In a skills competition, who do you think would experience the most stress: a professional golfer (PGA star Rickie Fowler), a club pro, or a total amateur who plays with his buddies on the weekends?

While I was a consultant with the Red Bull High Performance program, I sought to answer this question. Along with Dr. Leslie Sherlin, a neuroscientist, I devised a three-stage pressure test and measured each golfer's brain's neuroelectrical and heat rate activity during each stage of the test. We observed their biological data, and we asked questions to better understand the internal psychological strategies the golfers were using during the tests. During the first two stages, each golfer thought he was the only participant in the study.

Stage one was a low-pressure test: we placed eighteen golf balls around the green, ranging from one to fifteen feet from the flag, for each golfer to putt into the hole. I was alone with each golfer as they hit their putts. All the golfers demonstrated a slightly elevated heart rate and heightened brain activity.[1]

Fowler, the tour professional, not surprisingly made the most shots, holing fifteen out of eighteen. When I asked Rickie how he did, he responded, "I hit seventeen good shots." His math caught me a little off guard, and I said, "But only fifteen went in." Without missing a beat, Rickie said, "Right, but the way I think about golf is that I focus my attention on what's in my control, not on the end result. I committed to seventeen shots. I was seventeen out of eighteen." A nice glimpse into his mindset.

In stage two, we turned up the pressure by wheeling out two large cameras to the edge of the putting green and two hand-held cameras just a few feet from the golfers. We did not explain what the cameras were for or who the audience might be.

Fowler had an initial spike in heart rate and brain activation, but then quickly managed the over-aroused state and settled back down, with results similar to stage one. The weekend warrior had an increase in activation and performed slightly below when it was just the two of us on the putting green. He reported the experience as "fun" and "exciting" and that he "felt like a tour pro." He had no negative commentary about his performance.

The local club pro had a radically different experience. Not accustomed to playing in front of cameras, his heart rate spiked and stayed high for the duration of his turn. His results fell dramatically. "I was a mess out there. . . . I wish I had known you were going to film. . . . I looked like a fool. . . . I'm a professional. I'm supposed to do better than that."

In the final stage, all the golfers met each other for the first time. In addition to the cameras, we included two more pressure elements. We brought in an audience and made it a putting competition to raise money for a local charity.

The results were almost identical to the earlier stages. The PGA tour player used his mental skills to lower his heart rate, block out the external and internal noise, and regulate his emotional and physiological reactions. The weekend warrior viewed the experience as pure enjoyment and approached it with curiosity; he had nothing invested in the outcome. The club pro was the outlier. He performed poorly.

Why? He imbued the experience with much more meaning. Since he had overidentified with being "the expert," his identity was under threat. The combination of the cameras, the crowd, and the greater expertise of the tour pro amplified his fear of what others might be thinking about him: judging him a poor golfer, a fraud, not what he held himself out to be. And since he didn't have awareness of the thoughts that were triggering the cascade of chemicals driving him into a state of fight, flight, or freeze, he couldn't recalibrate.

He had been thrust into survival mode. On a golf course. On a sunny, seventy-six-degree day in Hobe Sound, Florida.

Wired for Protection

To understand our fear of people's opinions, we need a framework to understand fear.

Fear is an adaptive evolutionary response designed to keep us safe. The primary function of fear is to act as a signal of danger or threat and to trigger appropriate adaptive responses.

In ancient times, survival required an ability to rapidly identify and assess threat. Our hunter-gatherer ancestors were under pressure to outwit predators, defend themselves from invaders, and stay connected to the tribe. That was essential to their survival. Heightened vigilance and preparedness for things going wrong served our ancestors. They weren't penalized if they erred on the side of caution, but miscalculations could prove costly. If they fled from the proverbial tiger lurking in the woods, and it turned out to be a harmless animal, they only wasted a bit of time. But if they failed to pick up on the environmental cue, it could be at the expense of their lives.

The same principle held true socially. You couldn't go wrong attuning to the needs of the larger group, but if you fell out of favor with others and were excised from the tribe, that would likely be a death sentence. People could not survive on their own in a state of nature that was "solitary, poor, nasty, brutish, and short."[2]

The brain developed circuitry, supported by natural selection, that gave our early ancestors a heightened sensitivity to threat and, relatedly, a competitive advantage in the survival game. For millions of years the threat detection system carved deeply ingrained channels into the brain of early man.

Reflexes Are Not Just for Kicks

Fear is an emotion with physiological and cognitive components.

The threat reflex is an involuntary series of actions the body takes in response to a perceived threat—without us having to think about it. The stress response becomes activated in the brain and a predictable cascade of neurological and physiological events occur when we sense threat.

We can't have fear without having some of the following elements of the stress reflex. The moment we interpret something to be important, the amygdala, an almond-shaped structure on both sides of the brain, sends an alert to the hypothalamus, which switches on our sympathetic nervous system. Adrenaline gets released, raising our heart rate, pumping more blood, and triggering a massive release of glucose from the liver.[3] The blood vessels in our digestive system constrict, and blood gets redirected toward the muscles in the arms and legs so they can get ready to defend or spring away.[4] Our digestive process becomes marginalized. We don't need to digest food when we're under threat. Our stomach notices the shortage of blood and oxygen in that region, eliciting the oft-described feeling of "butterflies."[5]

The brain recognizes our body is working hard, and our cooling system gets activated as sweat begins to form on our skin. The moisture makes our skin more slippery and difficult to grab. While the vasoconstriction is happening and our heart is pumping harder, our breathing gets quicker and shallower. The increased blood flow to our extremities generates a feeling of heaviness in our legs and arms if our bodies are overactivated.

Our jaw clenches a little as the body is unconsciously preparing to bite, attack, or defend.[6] We reduce extraneous noise from the environment as our attentional focus narrows and we become more selective in processing sensory information. Increased muscle tension compromises our fine motor skills—things like finger movement and vocal cords—in favor of allocating resources to our bigger muscles.[7] That's why singing, playing the piano, archery, and public speaking can be so hard to do well when we sense a threat.

How Fears Are Learned

Understanding the biology and mechanisms on which fear is built is important to changing our relationship with fear.

The fear system is designed to keep us safe. The threat reflex is not particular to specific threats. It's generic in its response. We can essentially get fearful of anything if the circuit becomes activated.

The threat reflex can be activated at any time by two things: prior memories or immediate experiences, something that happens in the moment. The system embeds memories of previous experiences in us. Dr. Kerry Ressler, a professor of psychiatry at Harvard and one of the world's leading experts on the neurobiology of fear, says those memories can be protective or they can be dangerous.[8] Protective memories keep us from making bad choices or mistakes that could get us hurt. We avoid those dangerous situations in the future. The memory of swimming into twenty-foot surf in Hawaii when you had to be pulled out by a lifeguard protects you from putting yourself in that situation again. But other memories are dangerous because they circumscribe our behaviors in maladaptive ways.

Ring the Bell

Memories get embedded in our fear system through classical conditioning, also known as Pavlovian conditioning.[9] The Nobel Prize–winning Russian scientist, Ivan Pavlov, accidentally discovered that we learn through association in his now famous experiments on the digestion of dogs. Pavlov observed that the dogs would initially salivate only when food was placed in front of them, but he noticed that their physiological responses changed over time. They started salivating before the food arrived. Pavlov realized that the dogs were salivating in response to the noises that consistently accompanied the arrival of the food, like the sound of the approaching cart.

To test his theory, Pavlov set up an experiment where a bell was rung shortly before the food was delivered. Initially, the bells triggered no response in the dogs, but over time the dogs began to salivate at the sound of the bell by itself.

In the somewhat clunky parlance of classical conditioning, Pavlov used a "neutral stimulus," the ringing bell, that initially elicited no response from the dogs. The food was the "unconditioned stimulus" that led to an automatic response, the dogs salivating. The "conditioned stimulus" was the original neutral stimulus, the ringing bell, that after repeated associations with food elicited the same response.

Classical conditioning, a type of unconscious, automatic learning through association, is a mechanism through which we form fears.

In humans, an asymmetry exists between embedding positive and negative experiences. Humans don't require multiple pairings of a conditioned and unconditioned stimulus when something traumatic happens. Unlike Pavlov's dogs, which formed a new response after repeated pairings of the food and the bell, human fears can get formed in a single intense experience. An embarrassing social media post, a seventh-grade speech when you froze in front of the entire school, the discovery of a partner's infidelity, nearly drowning, the freefall of the financial markets where you've invested your entire savings—whatever the trigger may be—can create powerful fear in the moment. The fear sets in with a single experience and can last the rest of your life.[10]

This asymmetry is likely evolutionarily adaptive.[11] Throughout history, people who were better attuned to threats would have been more likely to survive and, consequently, would have increased probability of passing along their genes.

Embedded fears can of course also be integrated through multiple experiences over a long period of time. The girl who was continually excluded by her peers at school. The employee who endured an emotionally abusive supervisor.

The fear system, designed to anticipate problems and dangers to keep us safe, is primed for learning. The fear memory tends to become more generalized over time.[12] The long-term exclusion at school might evolve into a fear of intimacy. Or abuse in the workplace could morph into a broader distrust of authority.

No Magic Pill

The idea that we can take a magic pill that makes our fears disappear is seductive but not a reality. In fact, none of the current prescriptive treatments—like selective serotonin reuptake inhibitors (SSRI), Prozac, and Zoloft for depression, or beta-blockers to lower blood pressure—are based on the neurobiology of fear. They may reduce symptoms of fears but they are not tapping into a mechanism in the fear system.

There are a handful of psychological treatments that are commonly used to address maladaptive fear responses, with cognitive behavioral therapy (CBT) and acceptance and commitment therapy (ACT) leading the charge. A specific CBT intervention that has yielded meaningful results for intense fears is exposure therapy. This treatment involves a psychologist creating a safe environment so that when the client is exposed to the feared situation or object the client becomes either less sensitive to the anxiety-provoking condition or fully extinguishes the fear response altogether.

In my work as a sports psychologist, I've worked with athletes on this very issue. In fact, one person I've worked with was one of the best pitchers in baseball, a Cy Young Award–winner who, unbeknownst to most people, had a crippling anxiety about being criticized and judged by others.

We went through a process called systematic desensitization—a treatment that helps people deal with phobias by progressively exposing them to fear-inducing stimuli. The first step of the process was to understand how he experienced his fear. I needed to get a better sense of what it was like to be him. How did he identify with success and failure? How central was baseball to his identity? Did he experience increases in breathing and heart rate? Did he have the feeling of being unsettled? Did he have difficulty digesting food? Did he experience difficulty sleeping? Did his body feel tight? Or was he more overwhelmed with disruptive or constrictive thought patterns? Was he easily distracted? Did he catastrophize? Did his mind race? Was he indecisive? Was he forgetful?

He had a mix of both cognitive (mental) and somatic (physical) symptoms. He was "up in his head": overthinking his throwing mechanics, worrying about walking a batter, even obsessing over smaller decisions like what he wanted to eat for lunch. His anxiety also manifested in tension in his muscles, excessive sweating, and an elevated heart rate. For a pitcher who grips and throws a baseball ninety-eight miles per hour sixty feet and six inches into a small strike zone, sweaty hands, muscle constriction, and a racing heart are liabilities. His brain was secreting too many stress hormones and they were interfering with his ability to access his skills, in addition to lowering the overall quality of his life.

We explored the cost of the anxiety. It's important that someone really grasps the toll anxiety takes on their life. Talking about this toll allows me to see how much a client wants to change by doing the work. The commitment must be there because the work is difficult.

I told the pitcher, "I can create the structure for you to do the work, but you have to do the work. If you want to do it, then you can extinguish the fear." I offered encouragement: "You have the internal skills to transform your relationship with baseball and other areas of life. Rather than every trip to the mound being a referendum on you, you can bring a playfulness and freedom to the experience."

He instantly lit up with hope. His eyebrows went up. The corners of his lips turned upward. He took a deep breath and exhaled slowly. "Really? Can that really happen? This fear is awful."

I smiled, nodded, and asked him to share a time when he was on the mound "at his best."

He talked about his earlier days in professional baseball. "I remember thinking about the playing field as a canvas. This may sound strange but there was an artistic component to the experience. When I crossed the white lines, I felt like it was a place I could express myself. I had complete confidence in my ability. I had no noise. I felt connected to my teammates. I was a leader on the team but more by my actions than my voice. I loved baseball at that point in my life."

I shifted gears. "Do you want to have children?"

"Yup," he responded.

"Okay, let's imagine you have a fourteen-year-old boy, and he tells you he's 'going through something' and asks, 'Have you ever felt overwhelmed where you don't think you can get through it? Where part of you wants to quit because it's so over-whelming, and another part of you knows that you'd be leaving too early because there's so much more to explore?'"

He nodded.

"Can you see him looking into your eyes for help?"

"Yeah," he said, tearing up. "I had such intense anxiety the year after I won the CY Young. I was a mess at home, driving to the clubhouse, in the dugout. Everywhere. I was standing in the center of a stadium of fifty thousand people and all I wanted to do was hide."

"What do you want to say to your son about this moment in your life? There's no right or wrong answer. It's your life, your adventure, your fork in the road."

He leaned back into his chair, gathering his thoughts, qui-etly exploring all the options. He looked me in the eyes and said, "I just don't know if I can make it through this. I know what I want to say. I want to say, 'Yeah, I did the inner work. I faced my fears and found freedom in my entire life.' But I really don't know if I believe I can do it."

He went quiet. We just sat there in silence.

Finally, he spoke, "Yeah, I'm in. There's no other choice. I have to do this."

Now that we'd come to an understanding, we established a hierarchy of fear triggers, ranging from the weakest to the most terrifying. I had him outline from 1 to 100 the levels of fear that he felt. For level 1 (the smallest fear response), he wrote "getting in the car to drive to practice." Entering the locker room and seeing his name on the game-day lineup card was a 75. Walking onto the field for pregame warm-ups was an 85. The jog from the bullpen to the pitcher's mound was a 90. Being introduced by the public address announcer as the starting pitcher during postseason games pushed the fear meter to 100.

We then discussed the psychological skills that could help him work through his fears. We started with demystifying how psychology and physiology work together. We talked through why his body responded the way it does (as a protection and survival response). By the end of the overview, he was able to understand that his mind and body work together, and that at the most basic level, those responses are normal. At the same time, he recognized that in his profession, the chronic response of fear was completely maladaptive.

We moved to more concrete psychological training skills, like breathing training, mental imagery, optimism, self-talk, and cognitive restructuring strategies. The principle of mastering what's in one's control sits at the center of the work, so we shaped a plan that focused on those elements. We developed an optimized self-talk process. We built a set of relaxation strategies that included breathing training, to help downregulate his sympathetic nervous system (the fight, flight, or freeze mechanism designed to respond to acute stressors). We enhanced his mental imagery skills to make the images he visualized as lifelike as possible. The aim was to create as real an image as possible, ideally activating all five senses.

We also created a series of activities so he could intentionally "stress himself" in order to practice these controllable skills.

After a week of practicing these psychological skills, he was ready to begin the systematic desensitization training. Before we began, he agreed to a "contract" of sorts.

> I understand and agree that I'm about to purposefully face one of my fears. I understand the protocol is designed for me to experience multiple levels of fear, one at a time. I commit to deploying mental skills to work with my fear response and I commit, no matter how long it takes, to not leave the exercise while I'm in a fear response. I understand that doing so likely will result in intensifying my fear response. I am committing to working with each stage of fear until I can replace my fear response with a state of relaxation.

The contract demanded full commitment to a rite of passage that would enable him to earn the freedom he was working toward.

We agreed that the acceptable level of relaxation to move forward was a 2 out of 10 (with 10 being full-on panic, and 1 being boringly relaxed).

So, we began.

We pulled out the sheet on which he had listed his levels of fear. He cinched the strap tight on the heart rate monitor around his chest (so we could have some objective data, too) and I asked, "Are you ready?" He grinned, took a deep breath, and said, "Doc, you have no idea how ready I am to be done with this."

We both sat up a bit. He closed his eyes, as if signaling it was all business now.

I walked him through level 1 of his fear, using his imagination to feel what it was like to get into his car to go to the stadium. In less than twenty seconds, his breathing rate kicked up a notch, and his heart rate soon followed. His skin began to warm. In his mind, he was feeling exactly what it feels like to drive to the stadium.

"On our scale of 1–10, what's your level of activation right now?"

He replied, "6."

"Great. Use your psychological skills and go to work. Let me know when you are so relaxed that you feel as though you've mastered this level. Breathe. Smile—you're doing it."

He took a handful of deep breaths. The corners of his eyes and the corners of his lips turned upward. He was on his way.

A few moments passed, and he said, "I'm good. I'm totally chill."

His heart rate looked pretty close to his resting heart rate. I use that as a baseline for what "success" looks like at each stage of fear response.

The mechanics of systematic desensitization entail pairing the least frightening stimulus with the relaxation technique multiple times until the fear response diminishes. The process is based on a principle called "reciprocal inhibition" that posits that you cannot be anxious and relaxed at the same time. The maladaptive response gets replaced with an adaptive response. Conditioned effects of anxiety are inhibited by purposefully inducing a state of relaxation.

The intervention then moves to the next stimulus and then the next. The goal is to become gradually desensitized to the triggers causing the distress.

Once he developed command of each level using his imagination (technically called in vitro training), we mapped out a plan for him to apply the exact same structure, skills, and conditions, but this time, in real life (in vivo training). In this phase, he would get direct exposure to the feared situation in order to reduce fear and anxiety through firsthand experience. In vivo training aims to desensitize individuals to fear-inducing stimuli by gradually and safely exposing them to what they fear. This type of exposure therapy helps individuals overcome their fears, develop coping mechanisms, and regain a sense of control and confidence in the face of anxiety-provoking situations.

He nailed the real-life training.

In general, elite athletes are skilled at embracing discomfort. They recognize they need to get outside their comfort zone to learn, to get better. They often have a higher degree of comfort in new or challenging situations, a willingness to take risks, and a tendency to seek out novel experiences. Despite having a paralyzing fear, he was able to apply some of those traits he had developed to excel in sport to the challenges of in vivo training.

As a framework, he knew that if he could sit in the discomfort of the exercises long enough, despite them being taxing and exhausting, he could build a new mental model. And he did. The direct exposure to the stimulus desensitized him to the fear that had constrained him for so long. He extinguished the fear.

He could hardly believe it. He faced his fear, squared up with it, and changed his relationship with the game he loved.

A few days later he was in the lineup to pitch. When the announcer called his name, the camera locked on him as he entered the field from the dugout. Rather than taking what he called "the long walk"—for him what was always a dreaded walk from the dugout to the mound—he was lightly jogging with a big grin on his face. He had the freedom and buoyancy of a ten-year-old entering a Little League game. He even tipped his cap to the crowd.

He had unshackled himself from the social anxiety that had almost ended his career.

From Idea to Action

The fear of being judged by people has been measured for decades. Ronald Friend and David Watson developed the Fear of Negative Evaluation Scale (FNE) in 1969, a thirty-item, self-rated questionnaire designed to assess levels of social anxiety.[13]

We have designed an assessment to measure the fear of other people's opinions. FOPO, unlike social anxiety, is a nonclinical disorder. This is not a screening for social anxiety disorder or any other psychological disorder. If you are concerned you have symptoms of social anxiety disorder (SAD) that are interfering with your daily life, seek advice from a doctor or a mental health professional to see whether you meet the criteria for a diagnosis of SAD.

If you're interested in taking this assessment at no cost, please visit www.findingmastery.com/thefirstrule.

4

Identity:
A Breeding Ground
for FOPO

*The world will ask you who you are, and
if you don't know, the world will tell you.*

—**CARL JUNG**

Game 1. 1997 NBA Finals. Fourth quarter. 9.2 ticks on the clock.

Karl Malone, the league's reigning MVP, steps to the line for two free throws. His Utah Jazz, the best team in the West, are tied with Michael Jordan's Chicago Bulls, who are gunning for their second championship in a row—and their fifth in seven seasons—and their rightful place among the greatest dynasties in the history of sports.

The score: 82–82.

The game is in Malone's hands. He's an eleven-time All Star and a certain Hall of Famer. He'll go on to hold the record for the most free throws ever made, with a career success rate of 74 percent. If he sinks one of the two free throws, the Jazz will take the lead, and, barring some late MJ magic, win the game and steal home-court advantage from the unbeatable Bulls.

It's a moment that players dream about as kids. The NBA finals. The spotlight. The crowd. This is what all the practices, flights, sacrifices, and ice baths are for. To win a championship.

The Chicago crowd is rabid. "When Karl walked to the line, it was deafening in that stadium," recalled Brad Rock, a former sports columnist at *Deseret News*.[1] "My ears rang for days." The fans stand and scream and wave white wiggle sticks. But Malone is a total pro. Known as the Mailman, he always delivers—just like the Postal Service.

As Malone settles in, Scottie Pippen, the Bull's power forward—the quiet wingman to his trash-talking teammate, Michael Jordan—walks past Malone on his way to the blocks and addresses the man who would retire as the second-leading scorer in NBA history. "Hey, Karl," he says, "the mailman doesn't deliver on Sundays."

It's a perfect line—sharp and clever.

Malone goes through his normal preshot routine. He dribbles, head down, spins the ball in the air two times, crouches, rocks back and forth, says the name of his wife and daughter—and shoots.

Clank.

Miss.

82–82.

The crowd goes nuts. Malone walks away from the line and tries to collect himself. His face is pained with frustration and disappointment.

He walks back to the line. The crowd is so loud it drowns out Marv Albert, the play-by-play announcer for NBC. Malone goes through the same preshot routine as before. Dribble, spin, crouch, rock . . . shoot.

In and out.

Miss.

82–82.

No one can believe it. Malone, an all-time great, missed both shots.

The momentum shifts. After a television timeout, and with the same nine ticks on the clock, Michael Jordan takes an inbound pass, sizes up Jazz small forward Bryon Russell, and drains the game-winner as time expires.

The rest is history. The Bulls would go on to take the series in five games—and Scottie Pippen's trash talk would become a part of NBA lore.

There's no telling if Pippen's remark was the reason for Malone's missed free throws. Maybe Malone was tired after grappling in the post with Dennis Rodman. Maybe the pressure and the noise got to him. Or maybe, as others have speculated, his shots were affected by the bad court burn he suffered on his hand during the Western Conference Finals. Or maybe he just plain missed.

It's impossible to tell. We'll never know, because Malone followed a warrior's code: he never made excuses.

But the story fascinates NBA fans for a reason. Malone was an elite athlete, at the top of his game—a Goliath among Davids—who failed to deliver in a high-pressure moment on his sport's biggest stage. It was dramatic and devastating. And even more so because Malone, a big man who weighed 250 pounds, was knocked off balance by six simple words.

"The mailman doesn't deliver on Sundays."

Though most of us don't work in an environment as loud, intense, and stressful as an NBA Finals game, we've all been rocked and roiled by a parent or boss or teacher or coach or colleague that pierced through our emotional armor, leaving us exposed and vulnerable.

It begs the question Why are we so vulnerable to the targeted opinions of others? What hides behind the emotional armor?

What Is Identity?

As we saw with the club pro, identity is one of the most fertile breeding grounds for FOPO. Our identity, depending on how it's constructed, can leave us vulnerable to the slings and arrows of the opinions of others. When we have fused ourselves to an identity that is not true to who we are or to an identity that's too narrow to contain the whole of who we are or to an identity incapable of incorporating new information and growing, the opinion of another can feel like an assault where our survival is at stake.

If I'm the mailman who always delivers, what happens when I don't deliver? Who am I then?

Identity is our subjective sense of self built on our experiences, beliefs, values, memories, and culture. It's a set of physical and psychological characteristics that is not shared with anyone else. Often derived in relationship or comparison to others, identity provides a framework to better understand our place in a complicated social world.[2]

We have a natural impulse to define ourselves in relationship to the world around us, to give others a clear way to think about us. We construct identities because they help us better understand our place in a complex social world and reduce our subjective uncertainty.[3] Identity gives us something to grasp onto as we fall through the air. But the certainty that comes with "This is who I am" comes with a hefty price tag if we don't really understand who we are or if that label comes from outside ourselves.

Sources of Identity

Identity draws from many aspects of us—race, gender, sexuality, relationship, family, job, interests, nationality, beliefs, religious practices, and group affiliations—but it cannot be defined by any one of those aspects. Nor can it be solely expressed by any of the roles that sit inside those broader categories. Priest. CEO. Mother. Pilot. Writer. Student. Athlete. Entrepreneur. They are what we do, not who we are, though they inform our identity.

As Tyler Durden bluntly puts it in *Fight Club*, "You are not your job. You're not how much money you have in the bank. You are not the car you drive. You're not the contents of your wallet. You are not your fucking khakis."[4] You're just you.

Identity can morph over time based on the knowledge we gain about ourselves through experience and how we apply that knowledge in our lives. In Lewis Carroll's classic novel *Alice's Adventures in Wonderland*, the young protagonist goes down a rabbit hole into a fantastical world of anthropomorphic characters. After undergoing a succession of physical metamorphoses, she comes upon a caterpillar who asks, "Who are you?" Alice responds, "I—I hardly know, sir, just at present—at least I know who I WAS when I got up this morning, but I think I must have been changed several times since then."[5]

Embedded in identity is the idea that, despite physical and internal changes, there's a continuity between who someone was ten years ago, ten days ago, and today.[6] Take Jorge Mario Bergoglio. In his younger days, he worked as a bar bouncer, janitor, and a part-time technician, responsible for raw materials in a chemical lab in Buenos Aires. Today, he's based in Rome and leads an organization with 1.345 billion followers. Elected by the College of Cardinals in 2013 as the head of the Catholic Church, Bergoglio is now Pope Francis, a name he chose to honor St. Francis of Assisi.

Clearly, Bergoglio has changed. He's no longer the same person he was decades ago in Argentina, so what makes Mario Bergoglio Pope Francis? What is it that threads our past self to our present self and future self? What is the essential property that makes you "you"?

Boiled down to its bare essence, identity refers to how people answer the question "Who am I?"

Back in the Good Old Days

In earlier historical times, identity was not such an issue. To a large degree, when societies were more stable, identity was assigned and assumed. Living in smaller communities where people stayed in place, you knew who someone was. Part of their identity was often reflected in their name.

Last names began to be widely used in England after the Norman conquest in 1066. As the population grew, people needed to be more specific when they were talking about someone, so a last name was added. According to Richard II's poll tax lists, by 1381 most English families had embraced the practice of having a heredity surname.[7]

A group of British researchers did a six-year study that traced the origins of every surname shared by at least one hundred people in the United Kingdom in the 2011 census. Most names fell into one of four categories. The most common, locative names, described where one lived. The Underhills could be found at the base of the hill. Ford was at the river crossing. And the Atwaters lived down near the lake. The second largest grouping reflected occupation. Smith, the most common English name, worked with metal. Baker was, not surprisingly, the occupational name for someone who baked. The Archers were often professional bowmen. Patronymic surnames were usually based on the father's first name, letting people know who your father was. John Davidson was the son of David. The last category was English surnames derived from nicknames. Longfellow was the tall one at the end of the bar. Lilywhite didn't get out in the sun much. The Merriman family generally had a good disposition.

In our contemporary world, many of the traditional social sources of identity have weakened.[8] Globalization has undermined our shared national story and identification with country.[9] We are more mobile and less likely to stay in the communities in which we were known. A growing number of people no longer identify with a religious group.[10]

With the traditional sources of identity providing less help in answering the question "Who am I?" people are reaching for other alternatives. The modern world has given rise to new forms of self-identification.

Defining Who We Are by How We Do

We live in a performance-obsessed culture. A fixation with how well we perform has seeped into work, school, youth sports, even social media. The quality of our performance impacts how other people define us but, more significantly, how we define ourselves.

Human performance sits at the center of a paradigm shift that's taking place inside business. Enterprise organizations are moving away from a top-down model that raised productivity by extracting more out of employees to a performance model that looks to unlock human potential in the workplace. The shift is being driven by many convergent forces, but chief among them is the need for organizations to be innovative, fast, and agile in the face of a rapidly changing, unpredictable business environment. The central question leaders are asking is: "How do we create the internal and external conditions that people need to perform their best?"

Technology has leaped into the performance party. Driven by the adage "You can't improve what you can't measure," we now have performance metrics for almost everything we do. Digital devices and apps measure the substrata of human performance. Hours slept. Calories consumed. Time managed. Workflow. Productivity. Engagement. Well-being. Impressions. Followers. Likes. Comments. Social reach. Potential reach. Click-through rate. Breaths taken. Breaths held.

Performance is the central driver in an expanding youth sports industry that increasingly follows a professional sports model. Private coaches, relentless training, and intense early specialization have become the norm as parents push kids to get an early jump on the popular misconception that ten thousand hours of deliberate practice is going to pave their way to greatness, or at least to a college scholarship.[11]

The obsession with performance is reflected in popular culture. Podcasts offer signposts to finding mastery. Books unlock greatness codes, strip-mine wisdom from outliers, and reveal the tools of titans. Consulting giants promise to "equip people and organizations to unleash sustained performance." Celebrity instructors share their journeys, mindsets, and insights in online courses. Top-ten lists show us the shortcuts and hacks to the high-performance mountaintop, though, in reality, there are none.

Our culture obsessively celebrates individual excellence and performers who are skilled at specific activities and crafts. We once needed generalized skill sets to survive—to hunt, gather, grow food, construct dwellings, look after the family—but that has changed. The rise of technology opened the floodgates for specialization. People can now focus on that one thing. The social media expert. The stock market wiz. The influencer. The supernanny.

Basing One's Self-Worth on Performance Results

Rather than defining ourselves by what we do (professional identity) or where we do it (organizational identity), a performance-based identity is defined by how well we do something relative to others. When our identity is linked to performance, the quality of our performance defines who we are. We arrive at an understanding of who we are by comparing our performance results to others. *I'm better than the vast majority of people in* _____ (fill in the domain). We identify ourselves relationally. Developmental scientist and USC associate research professor Ben Houltberg, PhD, LMFT, who has extensively studied the motivations behind the pursuit of excellence, says a performance-based identity is defined by three factors: a contingent self-worth, a looming fear of failure, and perfectionism.

We think that if we perform successfully, then we'll feel good about ourselves. *If I get that book published . . . If I can close that deal . . . If I get that promotion . . . If I get through that to-do list . . . If I make the honor roll . . . If I'm the top sales agent again this year . . . If I get nominated for an Academy Award . . . If I win our local club tournament . . . If I win Wimbledon . . . If my social post goes viral. . . .* Our self-esteem becomes contingent on our performance and the outcome of the event. Achieving our performance objective provides only temporary relief, because just behind that performance lies the next one. Our self-esteem becomes the by-product of a series of "if-then" statements and we end up on a never-ending loop in pursuit of our self-worth.

The pursuit of excellence and high performance is important. We learn about ourselves by doing difficult things and testing the boundaries of our perceived limits. But when the core motivation of pursuing excellence is proving our self-worth, mistakes, failures, opinions, and criticism are experienced as threats rather than learning opportunities.

When our self-worth and value are based on the results of performance, it's far easier to play it safe by not trying. If who we are is based on what we do, then the doing becomes one of the greatest threats we face. We avoid situations we think we might fail. We lose the freedom to test ourselves and see what we are made of. Perfectionism is not driven by a healthy striving for excellence as much as it is an effort to avoid the negative judgment of others and the shame of not measuring up to our identity.[12] We long for acceptance and belonging but believe those needs can be met only if our performance meets or exceeds expectations.

People with high performance-based identities constantly ruminate and make assumptions about what other people think about them with little self-reflection. It's an almost automatic response or reaction. The assumptions are so implicit and quick that we react without considering whether the thoughts might be a by-product of our fear and insecurity.

Dr. Houltberg points out that identity does not operate just inside a person's domain of expertise. "It's a pattern of thinking that gets transferred to other areas."[13] It shows up in relationships. It plays out at work and in parenting. "If it's not dealt with, it cascades throughout your life to the point that you always feel like your worth and identity are based on your performance."

People who develop a performance-based identity do tend to perform well by objective measures, but the identity is buttressed by external validation. The praise and opinions of others fuel the identity. A performance-based model can work, but it's not sustainable. The exhaustive need to perform will tear at the seams of well-being, relationships, and one's own potential.

An individual's performance-based identity constitutes a core part of who they are to the point that if the identity were lost or destroyed, they would no longer feel completely themselves.

Performance-based identity is not to be confused with self-efficacy. Self-efficacy is a belief in one's ability to perform a certain task.[14] Performance-based identity is a belief about who you are based on the result of the task(s) performed.

Part of the allure of a performance-based identity, unlike other work identities, is that it's transferable. It can be carried across companies, and even across jobs, something that holds appeal in an era when we change careers and roles more frequently.

A House Built on Sand

Performance is meant to be an expression of who we are, not a definition of who we are. When we define ourselves by performance, we build our identity on a house of sand. How well we do at anything in life shifts and changes. Harnessing our sense of self to performance, and the approbation that comes with it, creates a petri dish for stress, anxiety, and depression.

Identity Foreclosure

What I've found troubling is when young people lock into a performance-based identity from an early age. In psychology, this is called identity foreclosure, a process where people prematurely commit to an identity before they have had a chance to explore and contemplate all the options. Ages twelve to eighteen are critical identity-formation years. That's the period when we begin to figure out who we are. We try out some different types of music. We try out new friends. New activities. New interests. We investigate new ideas about ourselves.

Instead of going through that process, I see so many talented young athletes, artists, and students who stop exploring their identity and identify themselves with that activity that brings them praise. When someone asks a young athlete or celebrity for an autograph or to take a photo because of what they do, how they look, or how well they perform, it can create confusion as to how they provide value to the world. "I am an athlete" might be one of the most seemingly benign, yet radically growth-limiting statements a young person can make. Their performance success becomes the basis of their identity. It's easy to understand how young, talented people foreclose on their identity. So much of their lives is devoted to that one activity. Many of their conversations during those early years are about how they did at practice, the last game, the performance, or at school. In the midst of normal adolescent confusion, the idea of locking in to a single, concrete identity can look very alluring.

Especially one that comes with a praise-based, dopamine-fueled spotlight. *I am an athlete. I'm a dancer. I'm a violinist. I'm an honor student.*

On the *Finding Mastery* podcast, I had a conversation with five-time Olympic gold medalist Missy Franklin about performance becoming the basis of one's identity.[15] Missy won a remarkable four gold medals and a bronze in her Olympic debut in 2012 when she was just seventeen years old. Her parents had been very conscientious of the value of making sure she had a broad base for her identity. "I was never just Missy the swimmer. I was first and foremost Missy their daughter. And then I was Missy the friend. And then Missy the swimmer, Missy the student, Missy whatever it was. They made sure that I knew I had so much more to offer this world than just what I could do in a swimming pool."

When performance slips, the edifice crumbles. When the spotlight goes off. When the praise quiets down. When someone else steps onto the podium. The over-indexed identity becomes exposed. Though Missy won a gold medal in the Rio Olympics four years later, her overall performance did not match the previous Olympic games. "For the first time I truly failed and had to experience that. I realized how much of my own self-identity and self-worth I had put into swimming and so when that was taken away, my world was totally rocked." That's coming from someone whose parents were incredibly intentional about not limiting her identity. Identity foreclosure is a slippery slope, even for people who are very discerning.

When we have early success, it's easy to get confused about how we provide value to the world.

Self-Protection

When we put our whole worth into performance, we will, of course, go to great lengths to protect the image we have of ourselves. As Dr. Houltberg notes, "One of the most significant consequences of performance-based identity is that it requires people to devote cognitive and behavioral effort to maintaining their identity in the face of asymmetries."[16]

A performance-based identity is prone to episodes of unconscious self-sabotage. We set ourselves up for failure to avoid finding out whether we would have failed. We build in an excuse for ourselves in the event the results don't meet our expectations.

For example, you spend days preparing for a big presentation, but you have a couple of loose threads that are needed to tie it all together. Rather than complete the final details of the preparation and walk in completely confident, you have a big night out with your friends on the eve of the meeting. When the presentation does not go as hoped, you blame it on your night out. You tell your friends, and yourself, "I should not have gone out last night. That was a huge mistake." Buried in the subtext of your admission is the implication that you would have performed well, but your choice undermined your performance. Your judgment may be brought into question but not your ability to perform. You will have never tested yourself, or at least that's how it appears. You will have chosen to preserve your identity rather than use the presentation as an opportunity to discover something about yourself, to see if you have the requisite skills to meet the challenge.

Other strategies are employed to mitigate the threat to the performance-based identity. We discount the source of the opinion. We attack or criticize the person we feel criticized by in an effort to discredit them. We respond with rationalization and a selective assessment of the evidence. We build counter-arguments. We ignore the information that runs counter to our own beliefs. The strength of these responses depends on how close that opinion comes to the heart of our identity.

A performance-based identity is not sustainable over time. Our ancient brains are hardwired to detect threats in our environment, but they are not very good at distinguishing between threats to our physical self and our social self. When our self-worth is tied to our performance, just the anticipation of the performance can trigger the same sympathetic nervous system reaction as if there were a tiger in the brush. The chain of rapidly occurring reactions inside the body, designed by nature to mobilize us to deal with threatening circumstances, deplete us by the time the game starts or the presentation is delivered. We are not designed to be fleeing from saber-toothed tigers ten hours a day, but that's what we are doing when our identity is anchored in our performance.

A House Built on Rock

The single greatest bulwark against FOPO is a having a strong sense of self. Know who you are and the opinions of others cease to be a constant threat. We want to build our identity on who we are, not what we do, not how well we do it, not who we do it with, and not where we do it. As Joseph Campbell put it, "The privilege of a lifetime is being who you are."[17]

To lay the foundation for a strong sense of self, the prime dictum is to not focus on the self. The way through FOPO is not thinking less of yourself but thinking of yourself less often. FOPO is self-referential. Our attention is directed at ourselves. To counterbalance that, we can shift our attention away from ourselves by making a fundamental commitment to learning and purpose. This leads to an entirely new way of experiencing ourselves and the world around us.

Learner's Mindset

Integrate discovery into your sense of self. Doing so gives you the internal space to grow and change and the freedom to be wrong or acknowledge what you don't know. Given that each moment is entirely brand-new, we want to build a psychological framework that allows us to discover the essence of each unfolding moment. A learner's mindset. To inhabit a learner's mindset, we need to let go of what we "know" to make room for what we don't know. A Zen parable captures the idea.

> A student came to a renowned monk and asked to learn about Zen Buddhism. Shortly after the monk launched into his discourse, the student interrupted him and said, "Oh, I already know that" in an attempt to impress the monk.
>
> The monk suggested they discuss the matter over tea.
>
> When the tea was ready, the monk poured the tea into a teacup, filled it to the brim—and then continued to pour—spilling tea over the sides of the cup and onto the table.

The student watched the overflowing cup until he could no longer restrain himself, "Stop! You can't pour tea into a full cup."

The monk set the teapot down and replied, "Exactly. Return to me when your cup is empty."

Anchoring our sense of self in discovery is not a cop-out to avoid committing to who we are; rather, it's simply an acknowledgment that we change with time. Everyone changes over time. I am not the same person I was when I started writing this paragraph. You will not be the same person you are now by the time you read the end of this paragraph. That's not a reflection of the words on the page, but the reality that we are continually changing. It's important to recognize that who we are at this moment is not the end point for who we are becoming. As Harvard psychology professor Dan Gilbert points out, "Human beings are works in progress that mistakenly think they're finished."[18] At each point in our life's journey, we tend to imagine that who we are at a point in time is the person we'll be for the remainder of our lives, a misconception Gilbert calls the "end of history illusion."[19]

Gilbert and his colleagues did a series of studies where more than nineteen thousand participants were asked how much they had changed over the previous ten years and/or how much they thought they would change in the coming decade. People, regardless of the stage of life, reported changing more in the previous ten years than they would have imagined a decade earlier. But they also believed that pattern of change was ending. Whether eighteen or sixty-eight years old, participants believed they would grow and change relatively little in the future; hence, the end of history illusion.

The tendency to believe that we've arrived at the person we are going to become has implications for our sense of self. The belief that "this is who I am right now and I'm a work in progress" is qualitatively different than "this is who I am." The latter gives rise to a rigid, fixed identity that is more susceptible to FOPO.

Rather than avoiding the discomfort that comes when people's opinions challenge our identity, we can learn to embrace them. To be curious about the origin of the ideas. We can train ourselves to hold those opinions up in the light, to look for the truth in them. To be curious about the opinion giver and explore how we can learn from the opinion. Curiosity does not always feel good, but it's a mark of growth.

After spending over two decades working with world-class athletes, artists, and leaders of industries, it is evident to me that they spend more time in the discomfort zone than others. They stay in it when it's hard, and they don't create excuses to move away from the emotionally charged experiences.

You can practice that same skill when someone's opinion trips an anxiety wire (or in any moment you feel challenged). Smile, breathe, and lean in. You're in it, and that space is where the discoveries happen. Rather than just trying to escape the intensity, take a moment to explore the landscape while you're there. Over time, the feedback of others, regardless of whether it's on point or misses the mark, becomes an opportunity to clarify who you are. This stress-embracing approach to life helps build incredible internal capacity and, over time, the strain and pressure strengthen our ability to be at home with ourselves in any environment, under any circumstance.

Nature offers up a metaphor for how stress and strain build strength.

In 1991, eight people went into a futuristic, airtight, three-acre miniature Earth called Biosphere 2 to study sustainability. Located in Oracle, Arizona, it was a real-life precursor to the closed system in the Matt Damon film *The Martian*. The planning and construction of the project took seven years. The natural environments inside included a rainforest, a grassy treed savanna, a desert, wetlands with mangrove trees, and a coral reef in a 25-foot-deep, 150-foot-long ocean.

Biosphere 2 faced many challenges, but one perplexing mystery was the toppling trees. Trees grew faster inside the domed space, but they would collapse before reaching their full height. The scientists were baffled until they realized that they had failed to include the natural element of wind. Trees need wind to strengthen their root system. The wind sways the tree trunk and puts tension on thin parts of the roots, causing them to splinter and grow deeper. It's why a planted tree should have only enough support to allow it to stand upright. The top of the tree needs to sway and move in the wind to build a strong trunk and root system.

Value Purpose above Approval

From a young age, we are conditioned to seek approval. That conditioning gets carried forward into adulthood, where we seek approval from bosses, spouses, friends, and colleagues. Over time, we develop a built-in mechanism to check outside ourselves to see if everything is okay. But we are not limited to that reflexive system. We have another choice: purpose.

Purpose is the belief that you are alive to do something. It is an internally derived, generalized intention that's both meaningful to you and consequential to the world beyond you. In short, your purpose matters to you. It has intrinsic value to you. It's bigger than you. And purpose has a future orientation.

Rather than looking outside ourselves to see if others approve, we can rewire that mechanism to turn inward and check against our purpose. "Am I being true to my purpose?" becomes the new reference point rather than "Am I being liked?"

Purpose, rather than approval, becomes the filter through which we make decisions, establish priorities, and make choices. We check in to see whether our thoughts and words measure up to our purpose.

On the surface, the objective of competition—whether sport or business—is to win. But those individuals or organizations that consistently win—and do it over a long period of time—tend to be driven by something more than the podium or the stock price. Purpose is not a prerequisite for high performance, but when our lives are anchored in purpose, we have more resilience in the face of challenges.

When something matters to us, we'll do whatever it takes. That's true for a loved one. That's true for an idea. That's true for the life that you want to live. We don't care what we look like or what other people think about us. We are deeply connected to what we are doing in the present moment.

Purpose, as described by Ben Houltberg, is a powerful motivator that organizes our sense of identity around what we value the most. Leonard Hamilton, the basketball coach from Florida State University, wrote a letter to legendary announcer Jim Nantz that shows what it looks like when purpose is embedded in our identity:

> I don't ever have a bad day. The measure of how I want to be remembered as a coach goes way beyond wins and losses. I want to see my players turn out to be good fathers, good husbands. It's a victory when I get to see them later on as leaders of their families. That's the record I care about. When they call me and tell me they're getting married, when they invite me to their wedding, when they ask me to be the godfather of their first child. Those are wins I care about.[20]

For people with a purpose-based identity, it's not the evaluation of other people that drives them or fuels them. It's the meaning of what they're doing and the potential of what they can impact.

Those are two very different fuels. One is sustainable, and the other will burn you out.

From Idea to Action

You can use any situation to practice decoupling your identity from the approval of others by mapping that situation against your core values. Core values are fundamental beliefs, guiding principles that dictate your behaviors.

Jot down five core values and then see how they hold up in a situation where your identity feels threatened. To illustrate, let's say creative expression is one of your core values. Your company has an upcoming black-tie event, but you want to wear a purple blazer. You know people are going to have a reaction to it. You start to get in your head, *My colleagues are going to think I'm inappropriate or I'm attention seeking.* At that point, you tap the brakes and say, *Hold on. Is my core value creative expression or do I default to what other people think?* Use that tension to map FOPO (*What are they going to think of me?*) up against your core value. Then you can make an informed decision. Maybe you decide, *Okay, my first principle is creative expression, but the company event is not the right time to express it.* Or you throw caution to the wind and break out the purple blazer.

If you are clear on your core values, each time the threat of someone else's opinion surfaces, you have a mechanism to run it through. This approach takes you out of the repetitive, ruminative FOPO loop (*What will they think?*) and replaces it with a measured response that brings your principles into clear focus. It shifts the focus to the content of the experience, rather than being a referendum on your identity, and gives you the power of conscious choice.

5

Outsourcing Self-Worth

*A man cannot be comfortable without
his own approval.*

—**MARK TWAIN**

In August 2017, Hillary Allen was close to finishing her PhD in neuroscience, and she was also ranked number one in the world in skyrunning, which is basically high alpine mountain running but with a focus on elevation gain and technicality. If trail running goes around the mountain, skyrunning goes up and down it. It's the equivalent of running an ultramarathon up a mountain.

On summer break from teaching college science classes, Hillary had gone to Europe to race for three months. As she recounted on the *Finding Mastery* podcast, she was midway through the final race of the summer in Tromsø, Norway, in the Arctic Circle. Running across a ridge, she spotted a photographer who was waiting to take her photo as she turned the corner on a technical section of the race. His nickname for Hillary was "Smiler" because she was always smiling, even when she was in pain. She said, "Hi Ian." He replied, "Just smile big for me around this corner." That was the last moment in the race she remembers.

She stepped on a loose rock and slipped off the edge of a cliff. The horizon flipped upside down and she grasped at air. She heard her own voice telling her to take a deep breath, that she was going to die and to remain calm because it would soon be over. Hillary fell 150 feet, bouncing off the mountain several times before her body came to rest on a vertical, inhospitable section of rock. She broke fourteen bones, including both her feet, both wrists, vertebrae L-4 and L-5 in her back, and five ribs.

A racer who had seen her fall risked his own life to climb down to reach her. She had open wounds and was covered in blood. He didn't think to check for vital signs. He thought he was recovering a body. Hillary's chest heaved and she regained consciousness. The first words out of her mouth to her rescuer were "Am I going to be okay?"

While Hillary's response in a moment of crisis is completely normal given the circumstances, it also illuminates the reflexive checking in with others to gauge how we are doing.

The desire to know that we are okay shows up in every area of life where uncertainty lurks. The delivery room. The boardroom. The bedroom. The classroom. When we are scared, unsettled, and confused, we either look inside ourselves for the answer or outside ourselves to the perceived authority, to the opinions of others. Whether we turn inward or outward to answer the question—or whether we even ask the question

"Am I okay?" at all—is ultimately determined by one thing: self-worth.

Self-Worth

Self-worth is our sense of value as a human being. It describes the core beliefs we have about our worth and value. Our self-worth is an internal measurement. It's how we see ourselves and who we perceive ourselves to be. Where we derive, and how we think about, our self-worth dramatically impacts our susceptibility to FOPO. People differ in what they believe they must be or do to have worth or value.

William James, considered the father of American psychology, wrote, "Our self-feeling in this world depends entirely on what we back ourselves to be and do. It is determined by the ratio of our actualities to our supposed potentialities. . . . So the seeker of his truest, strongest, deepest self must review the list carefully, and pick out the one on which to stake his salvation."[1] James believed self-esteem was based on two elements: our achievements and our aspirations. He demonstrated this idea in a simple mathematical formula:

$$\text{Self-esteem} = \frac{\text{Successes (achievements)}}{\text{Pretensions (goals)}}$$

How we feel about ourselves, according to James, can be boosted in two ways. We can achieve more—raise the numerator in James's formula. Or we can adjust our aspirations for the selves we want to be by selecting more modest but more relevant goals in the areas by which we define ourselves.

Following James's lead, Jennifer Crocker and Connie Wolfe introduced the construct "contingencies of self-worth" to describe the areas in which we base our personal worth and value.[2] The idea is that the self-worth is a judgment about the self, so it must be based on some criteria. People choose different areas to stake out their self-worth, depending on their objectives in the world. In their longitudinal study of 642 college freshmen, Crocker and Wolfe established seven different domains where students were most likely to stake their self-worth. Five of the areas were external: appearance (how attractive the individual feels in the eyes of others); academic competence (the ability to meet personal goals for scholastic achievement); competition (bettering others); approval from others (how other people evaluate the individual); and family support (compliance with what the family wants the student to do). Two areas were internal: God's love (the love and acceptance of God) and virtue (internalized ethical standards).

Our judgment about our own self-worth is contingent upon the outcomes in those areas. One person's self-worth might be contingent upon academic competence while someone else's might be conditioned upon how attractive that individual feels in the eyes of others or upon the love and acceptance of God. Global feelings of self-worth depend on the perceived success or failure in those areas on which self-worth is contingent. Success means I not only closed the deal but I am worthy and valuable.

We only make judgments about ourselves in those areas where we have planted our self-worth flag. That's why two people could have vastly different reactions to the same experience. Getting a B on a math exam could be a devastating experience for someone whose worth is anchored in academics, but that same B might be shrugged off by a friend whose self-worth is not contingent upon scholastic outcomes.

For the study, Crocker surveyed the students before they started college about the basis for their self-worth, and twice near the end of the school year.[3] More than 80 percent said academic competence, 77 percent said their family's support, 66 percent said doing better than others, and 65 percent said their appearance.

The study revealed the costs of students looking for external validation of their worth or value. The data showed that basing self-worth on external sources, such as academic performance, appearance, and approval of others negatively impacted physical and mental health. The instability of having self-worth dependent on external validation led to higher stress, more anger, relationship difficulty, and lower academic performance. Those students also had a greater tendency toward drug and alcohol use and more symptoms of eating disorders. By contrast, the students who based their self-worth on internal sources (religious faith and virtue) performed better in school, had lower stress, and less of a tendency toward drug, alcohol, and eating disorder symptoms.

Externalizing our self-worth, when it works, can yield short-term benefits. We get emotionally and chemically rewarded when we succeed. Our hypothalamus produces dopamine, often referred to as the feel-good neurotransmitter. Our self-esteem gets lifted, leaving us feeling safe, secure, and superior.[4]

But dependency on external validation and social approval has a dark alter ego that reveals itself over time.

The Price of Conditional Self-Worth

Psychologists Richard Ryan and Ed Deci's widely accepted self-determination theory (SDT) signaled a Copernican shift in our understanding of human motivation, upending the dominant belief that people were primarily driven by external rewards. SDT holds that human beings are driven by three basic internal needs that must be fulfilled to perform optimally and to experience well-being. They need to feel capable and effective in meeting the demands of the environment (competence). They need to feel a sense of belonging and a sense that they matter to others and others matter to them (relatedness). Lastly, they need autonomy, the freedom to make choices that align with their priorities, beliefs, and values.

Autonomy in this context does not mean independence; it means having volition and control. It's when people choose to do something because of the inherent satisfaction it yields. If people are interested in and enjoy an activity and choose it freely, they turn out to be better problem-solvers, more creative, more engaged, and more resilient in the face of challenges.

Outsourcing our self-worth undermines those basic human needs.

The effort required to maintain and protect conditional self-worth compromises your ability to form strong relationships. When your self-worth is contingent upon success or failure in a particular area, your primary drive often becomes proving to yourself, and others, that you meet those conditions of worth. As Crocker points out:

> The person whose self-worth depends on being smart or competent often needs to prove that others are less smart or less competent; the person whose self-worth depends on being kind and compassionate implicitly requires that others be less kind and less compassionate. For how can I convince myself and others that I am smart or good if you are smarter or better than I am? Thus, in seeking self-esteem we not only need to be competent, right, or good—we need to be more competent than others, right "over" them, or "more good" than they are.[5]

The focus on the self through the eyes of others—*What are others thinking of me? How am I performing?*—hinders our ability to attune to and be responsive to the needs of others.[6] Rather than turning outward to connect, we turn inward to defend or attack. Multiple studies have shown that when our self-worth is under threat, we respond by blaming others, withdrawing, making excuses, and expressing anger or aggression, further damaging the relationship.[7]

When our sense of self-worth is challenged, we instinctively tend to disregard or downplay feedback in order to protect ourselves. In doing so, we lose access to information about choices and responses that might enable us to improve upon what we are doing. Rather than actively working toward achieving our goals, we become fixated on avoiding unfavorable outcomes.

Perhaps above all, contingent self-worth empowers people's opinions about us at the expense of our own and undercuts the basic human need for autonomy. We expend an enormous number of resources looking outward to see if we are okay. We feel more controlled by what other people do, think, and feel. We give up our own ability to reassure ourselves. We have difficulty making decisions and commitments because we look for an answer outside ourselves rather than first looking within. We crowdsource our sense of self. We allow other people to decide how we feel about ourselves. The degree to which we empower the opinions of others varies depending on the environment, situation, and the domain of worth in which our identity is anchored.

When our worth is contingent upon the outcomes in a domain we have deemed important, we have signed up for a life of anxiousness and vigilance. Like our tribal ancestors, we live under the constant threat of attack, but it's not our physical safety we are safeguarding. We are protecting our self-worth.

We scan our environment with the situational awareness of Jason Bourne, Matt Damon's character from the *Bourne Identity* film franchise. We identify all the exits. We closely observe people, taking note of nonverbal clues. The goal is to be able to predict the actions and responses of others. Sometimes we strike preemptively before an opinion is expressed. We share a creative thought in a meeting by hedging our bet to soften the blow if it's not received well. "This may be a bad idea but what if . . ." Other times we shapeshift *after* an opinion has been lobbed into the bunker where our self-worth resides. When our boss does not immediately embrace our proposal, we quickly surrender our point of view and enthusiastically support an idea we don't like.

Our stress response is on high alert—and it rarely shuts off. Our nervous system does not know the difference between a rival tribesman wielding a spear and a supervisor giving us constructive but hard to hear feedback. As neuropsychologist Rick Hanson points out, "What's also natural, though—and you see it in the wild—is that most stressful episodes are resolved quickly, one way or another. The natural biological, evolutionary blueprint is to have long periods of mellow recovery after bursts of stress."[8] Protecting the domain in which our self-worth is staked exposes us to chronic stress because we are continually bombarded with threats, real and misinterpreted.

By externalizing our self-worth, we find ourselves in a never-ending loop in pursuit of it. We become trapped when our self-worth is a consequence, rather than the cause, of personal achievement. In this construct, our self-worth is sustained by successes and achievements and continually threatened by obstacles, failures, and the opinions of others.

How Did We End Up Here?

We have been conditioned and, in some cases, explicitly taught to value ourselves based on conditions that we must meet to win the love and positive regard of others. We enter the world completely dependent on our caregivers. A newborn giraffe calf is six feet tall and can stand up and run within an hour of being born. For the first two months of life, a human baby can barely lift its head without help. It's more than a decade before people have the ability to survive on their own. In our early years, we observe what pleases our caregivers—what behaviors are rewarded and those that are not—and we follow suit.[9] We watch our caregivers with wide eyes to figure out what we need to do (and not do) to be taken care of. We learn from a very early age that the responses of others have a direct impact on our well-being.

A caregiver's conditional regard is often a way of socializing children, and it can dramatically impact a child's self-worth. An adult can provide love and affection when their children exhibit certain positive behaviors or attributes. They lavish praise for successes and the child meeting the conditions that have been set for them. Conversely, affection gets withdrawn in the wake of an undesired behavior or outcome. The rupture induces anxiety in the child and motivates a behavioral change that, in turn, gets rewarded with affection and reduces the anxiety.[10]

Children can receive messages from their parents that their level of worth and appreciation is dependent on exhibiting certain behaviors or being a certain way. The subtext is that they are not good enough for their parents as they are. Something else is required to be worthy.[11] Children often internalize the idea and come to believe they are not good enough for anyone, including themselves.[12]

Wider culture reinforces the messaging of conditional self-worth. A competitive academic world leads students to believe grades and standardized test scores are a measure of their value. Advertisers seek out consumers' pain points, creating problems that did not exist to sell them products they don't need.[13] Social media drives social comparison with carefully curated, idealized images, measuring our value in followers, likes, shares, and comments.

We are raised on a steady diet of other people's opinions, judgments, and perceptions. Along the way, we may be taught to think critically and discern for ourselves, but well-grooved preverbal habits are incredibly hard to break.

We absorb and interpret messages from our environment and transmute them into behaviors that we believe are socially acceptable. Over time, that pattern of behavior informs our relationship with our friends, teachers, partners, and supervisors.

Inherent Value

Legendary British ad man Rory Sutherland said, "Engineers, medical people, scientific people, have an obsession with solving the problems of reality, when actually most problems, once you reach a basic level of wealth in society, most problems are actually problems of perception." He was making a case that advertising adds value by changing the perception, not the product—and that perceived value can be just as rewarding as real value.[14] In essence, we can change behavior by telling people a story that makes them perceive something differently. He could easily have been talking about solving the problem of conditional self-worth.

You could overcomplicate the solution and talk about all the changes you need to go through to liberate yourself from the resource-draining, unstable, and limiting prison of conditional self-worth. You could go through regression therapy and get a better understanding of how your early-life caretakers gave you implied messages of contingent worth. You could sift through the wreckage of emotional or physical suffering you endured growing up. But it's not that complicated.

You simply need to recognize that you are worthy exactly as you. You are not your grade—whether it's an A or an F. You are not your job, your age, your marathon time, your place on the org chart, your relationship status, your gold bars, or your prison bars. You have inherent value, and it's not conditioned on anything you do or have done. It's not conditioned by how virtuous you have been or how many mistakes you've made. Your virtue and your failures are not factored into the calculus of your value as a human being. Your value stems from your being, not your doing.

From Idea to Action

Develop an awareness of where your self-worth is externally anchored. Where are you externalizing your sense of value? What are the domains in which you need to meet standards in order to feel worthy? There does not have to be one single domain where your self-worth is staked; it could be scattered across a few. Ideally, self-worth is not conditional, but explore the following areas to better understand your orientation.

Social approval	My self-worth is contingent upon being accepted, appreciated, and validated.
Workplace	My self-worth is contingent upon a standard of performance at work.
Money	My self-worth is contingent upon the perception of financial wealth.

Academics	My self-worth is contingent upon scholastic achievement.
Appearance	My self-worth is contingent upon meeting cultural standards for attractiveness.
Social comparison	My self-worth is contingent upon being "better" than others in a given area.
Virtue	My self-worth is contingent upon being a virtuous person.
Parenting	My self-worth is derived from my child's accomplishments and well-being.
Power	My self-worth is contingent upon my sense of power.
God's love	My self-worth is contingent upon God's love.
Family approval	My self-worth is contingent upon compliance with my family's desire.

Knowing where you have staked your self-worth can help you better understand what motivates your behaviors and responses, and help you develop a greater awareness of your areas of psychological vulnerability.

6

The Neurobiology of FOPO

*I know but one freedom and that
is the freedom of the mind.*

—ANTOINE DE SAINT-EXUPÉRY

Alone with Our Thoughts

"I don't have any time for myself." A common lament, or boast, in a culture where busyness has replaced leisure time as a status symbol. We signal both our fatigue and our social worth in a single declarative sentence. We imply that scarcity and demand make us desired human capital, but our lives would be better if we had time by ourselves.

It's a nice thought, having more time to ourselves. But, as University of Virginia psychology professor Timothy Wilson and his colleagues discovered, many of us hate being alone with our thoughts and would go to shocking lengths to avoid doing so.[1]

Wilson's team asked college students to spend time alone in a stripped-down room and entertain themselves with their own thoughts. The only rules were they had to remain in their chairs and stay awake. Afterward, participants answered questions about how much they enjoyed the experience and whether it was difficult to concentrate.

Most previous research in this area had focused on people trying to engage in an external task (like reading) and their minds involuntarily drifting away. In those cases, people were generally happier when their minds stayed engaged in the task. Without anything in the room to compete for their attention, one might guess that the participants in Wilson's study would be able to occupy their minds with positive, engaging thoughts. But that wasn't the case.

Most participants reported that it was difficult to concentrate and their minds wandered. The majority of the students did not enjoy the experience of being inside their own heads.

The researchers took it a step further to test how resistant people were to being alone with their thoughts. Once again, the students were put in a room (alone) with no stimuli and asked to entertain themselves with their thoughts. This time, they were given the option of pushing a button that would give them an uncomfortable electric shock. (All the participants had previously experienced the shock and said they would pay money to avoid it.) It was clear they would rather do something than be alone with their thoughts, but would they rather engage in an unpleasant activity than no activity at all?

The results showed that many people would. Twenty-five percent of the women broke up their thinking time with an electric shock, while a whopping 67 percent of the men chose to shock themselves at least once. One outlier pushed the button 490 times! Imagine being in that guy's head.

Why do we have such an aversion to being alone with our thoughts?

There's a Party Going On in Here

The answer may lie in the default mode network (DMN). No, that's not an electronic music band from the eighties.[2] DMN is a highly complex network of interacting regions in the brain that may be the neurological basis for our sense of self, the seat of suffering, and the source of FOPO. But that gives DMN a bad rap and I'm getting a little ahead of myself.

In the last sixty years, scientists have made quantum leaps forward in unraveling the mysteries of the brain using detailed imaging that maps neural networks. In the words of neurologist Marcus Raichle of Washington University in St. Louis, "The microscope and telescope opened up unexpectedly vast domains of scientific discovery. A similar opportunity has now been created in the study of human cognition by the introduction of methods to visualize the brain systems involved as we think."[3] No longer was a surgeon's knife needed to view the brain. Noninvasive functional magnetic resonance imaging (fMRI) technology has enabled scientists to safely gather insights about how the mind works.

For years, scientists focused on tracking changes in the brain when people were absorbed in an activity. No one gave much consideration to what goes on inside the brain when people are doing very little. Raichle shifted that paradigm in the 1990s.

Following the standard practice of brain-mapping studies, Raichle and his colleagues asked participants to do simple tasks, like reading words aloud, identifying colors in pictures, or trying to recall if a word appeared on a list they had been given earlier. The researchers then used an imaging technique, positron emission tomography (PET), to see where blood flowed in response to the brain activity.[4] They were looking for increases in brain activity associated with different tasks.

To measure the change, scientists would establish a resting baseline for the activity when the participants were in undirected mental states. In Raichle's laboratory, they typically required participants to look at a blank screen. One day, Raichle noticed that activity in certain regions of the brain was reduced when the subjects were engaged in demanding tasks. Even more surprising was that activity in these same areas increased when the task was completed. The brain seemed to revert back to a default activity level in the absence of a specific external task. The brain in these regions was busy when it was supposed to be at rest. Taken aback, Raichle wasn't sure what was going on, but he made a practice of tracking the phenomenon in all their experiments.

From that accumulated control data, Raichle accidentally discovered the default mode network (DMN), a never before seen, interconnected group of brain structures that, paradoxically, is more active when we are not engaged in an external task.[5]

Until Raichle's findings, the common assumption was that the primary function of the brain was to solve tasks and, if not engaged, the brain was freed up or passive.[6] It had not occurred to anyone that the brain is just as busy when we relax as when we concentrate on challenging activities.

The discovery partly explains why the brain uses almost as much energy "resting" as it does performing complicated mental tasks, and why the brain accounts for about 20 percent of the energy consumption in an average adult human, even though it only represents 2 percent of our body weight.[7] It turns out that the brain doesn't really shut off.

A Not-So-Idle Mind

Well, if the brain is always switched on, what is it doing when it's not explicitly focused on a goal? At the risk of oversimplifying, it slips into a pattern of activity that's the neural equivalent of mind wandering. The default mode network serves many purposes, but given nothing else to do, the brain often defaults to thinking about its favorite subject—the person it resides in.

The DMN is still not well understood, but the prevailing idea is that it's the hub for self-referential mental activity where we can drift into unproductive, repetitive, negative thinking. Dredging up memories. Worrying about the future. Judging oneself and others. Questioning the intention of others. Thinking about what others think about us. Fearing what others think about us.

For most people, the wandering mind is not a happy mind. That was the conclusion of a study by Harvard social psychology professor Dan Gilbert and Matthew Killingsworth.[8] They built an iPhone app and used it to contact more than five thousand participants from eighty-three countries at random times during the day. The participant was asked, "Are you thinking about something other than what you're currently doing?" and they were also asked whether that moment was pleasant or unpleasant.

The study found that on average we spend nearly 47 percent of our waking hours in a mind-wandering state. Almost half our lives we are thinking about something other than what we are doing. While that can be a positive diversion during moments of creative exploration, it creates an emotional toll when those thoughts lead us to feel dissatisfied and unhappy in our lives—and generally that's what happens when we perseverate on what someone else may or may not be thinking about us.

How do we reconcile the recognition that amazing things are born out of an unstructured, free-flowing, roaming mind, yet we feel better when our mind is not wandering? In truth, we need both. Our real power lies in being able to choose where to place our attention and having the mental skills to do so. To choose whether we want to ruminate on what our partner, colleague, classmate, coach, friend, or nemesis may or may not be thinking about us.

Our attention does not have to be hijacked by every passing thought we have about other people's perceived opinions of us. The meandering mind need not be the tail that wags the dog. How do we direct our attention where we want it to go rather than default to the brain's primitive craving for social approval?

Mindfulness.

Attention, Please

A number of scientific studies confirm what ancient Eastern traditions have known for centuries—training mindfulness can quiet the activity in the default mode network, the breeding ground for the monkey mind and ground zero for FOPO.[9]

Mindfulness is not new. For millennia, contemplative practices like meditation have provided a way to look inward and explore our mental and emotional processes. Only relatively recently did they find their way into the Western world. In the mid-1800s, Henry David Thoreau and Ralph Waldo Emerson were deeply influenced by the major works of Eastern spiritual traditions, but they did not have training in the practices that underpin the texts. Mindfulness started to get more attention in the 1960s as teachers from Asia and India came to the West and Westerners went abroad to learn the mysteries of the ancient Eastern internal arts.

Jon Kabat-Zinn, a man I deeply admire and whose mentorship has been valuable, reimagined mindfulness for a secular world while he was a graduate student at MIT in the 1970s. With a PhD in molecular biology, he recognized its health benefits and went to great lengths to anchor mindfulness in science to ensure that it did not get stigmatized as a new-age fad or esoteric Eastern mysticism.[10] He founded the Mindfulness-Based Stress Reduction (MBSR) clinic that teaches mindfulness meditation training for people with chronic pain and stress-related disorders.

Mindfulness is a foundational tool to change your relationship with FOPO. It enables you to be more aware of your thoughts, feelings, and emotions in each moment, giving you the space to respond rather than react. Mindfulness is both a state of being and a skill. It's the state of "awareness that arises from paying attention, on purpose, in the present moment and non-judgmentally."[11] Mindfulness is also a skill that can be employed to bring the practitioner into that state of awareness.

Mindfulness practice helps create space from our cognition and emotion so we can see things as they really are. We are able to recognize that we are not the thoughts we hold about ourselves. We are not the thoughts and opinions that others may or may not have about us. We are infinitely bigger and far more dimensional.

We don't need to go somewhere else to access our awareness. Awareness is always available. We just need to develop the mental skills to drop into it.

Broadly, there are two types of mindfulness practices. Contemplative mindfulness is simply about observing your thoughts without judgment. You watch how your inner thoughts and emotions work together. Single-point mindfulness places the focus of your attention on a single object, the most common being your breath. But the point of attention could be anything. A sound. A candle flame. A spot on the wall.

Mindfulness practice enables us to become more aware of how frequently our minds ruminate about what others may or may not be thinking about us. We begin to recognize the underlying worry that shapes so many of our thoughts and behaviors. We become more skilled at working with those thoughts. We start to identify the triggers, conditions, and thought patterns that drive our desire for social approval.

From Idea to Action

Practice mindfulness.

Sounds easy, but it's actually enormously challenging. Try single-point mindfulness for a couple of minutes and see what surfaces. If you are like most people, your mind will drift to the past, the future, or a thought that bubbles up about the present moment. Many of the thoughts are relational—in relationship to another person and oneself. A simple digital video call can turn into an inward journey to nowhere as our mind reflexively drifts. *This screen reminds me of the Hollywood Squares . . . Who was the host of that—Peter Marshall? . . . No one on this call is old enough to know that reference . . . Does it look like I have a double chin from that camera angle? . . .*

Your mind may hop on a "train of thought," a sequence of interconnected ruminations. A single thought is all that's required to get the train to leave the station. *I haven't seen a single one of my daughter's soccer games because I'm working all the time.* At each stop, the train picks up a new thought. *How do I have so little control over my life? Everyone else goes to the games and makes time for vacations. I work.* One thought leads to the next. *I'm a cog in a big machine disguised as a purpose-driven culture.* Once aboard, the train can take you a long way down some dark tracks before you realize you are not where you hoped or intended to be. *I need to find a new job.*

At some point, you will notice that your attention is no longer focused on your breathing. With the recognition, you let go of the thought that has pulled you away and direct your attention back to your focal point—the breathing. This cycle will repeat itself again and again.

The practice illuminates the mind's tendency toward distraction, along with its continual preoccupation with other people and what they might be thinking about you. With repetition, you more quickly notice when your attention has shifted off its point of focus. You become more skilled at navigating the mind and focusing your attention where you want it to go.

If you'd like to explore a few guided meditations, you can download them at www.findingmastery.com/thefirstrule.

PART TWO

ASSESS

7

Barry Manilow and the Spotlight Effect

*You will become way less concerned with
what other people think of you when
you realize how seldom they do.*

—DAVID FOSTER WALLACE

Cornell Professor Thomas Gilovich and his colleagues devised a social experiment, published in 2000, to see whether other people are really observing and judging us at every turn.[1] One hundred and nine college students entered a room full of their peers, individually and alone, wearing a T-shirt with a photo of the pop singer Barry Manilow emblazoned on the front. The researchers had selected an image of Manilow, the patron saint of uncool, knowing that it would be "embarrassing" for the students. Sorry, Barry.

The observers in the room were sitting at a table facing the door when the student walked in wearing the T-shirt with the pop star emblazoned on the front. After a short interaction, the student left the room and was asked by researchers, "How many of the students who were filling out questionnaires in the laboratory would be able to state who was pictured on your T-shirt?" The observers were asked, among other filler questions, if they noticed who was pictured on the shirt of the student.

As the researchers predicted, the students wearing the Manilow shirt dramatically overestimated the number of people who paid attention to what they were wearing. The subjects guessed that about 50 percent of the people in the room would take note of the image of Manilow. On average, less than 25 percent of the observers actually could recall the subject's shirt. When other students were asked to watch the videotape of the experiments and estimate what percentage of the room would remember the Manilow shirt, they correctly guessed around 25 percent. The simple act of wearing the shirt in front of their peers dramatically elevated their perception of how much attention was being placed upon them.

The phenomenon, dubbed the "spotlight effect," describes how people overestimate the extent to which their actions and appearance are noted by others.[2] We tend to believe that others are paying more attention to us than they actually are.

In fact, we pay a lot more attention to ourselves than other people pay to us. We think we are "in the spotlight" and all eyes are observing our every move, and our shortcomings are getting magnified for all the world to see.

Why?

Underlying the phenomenon is an egocentric bias. We live at the center of our own worlds. We are acutely focused on our own behavior and appearance, and we tend to believe that other people are equally focused on us. That doesn't imply we are self-absorbed and arrogant. Rather, our worldview is a product of our own experiences and perspective, and we attempt to understand other people's thoughts and actions through that same lens. It can be difficult to accurately assess how much or how little other people are focused on us.

We overestimate how much other people pay attention to both our negative and positive actions. There's often a wide chasm between how we view something we've done and how other people view it. As the researchers noted:

> Whether making a brilliant point in a group discussion, contributing to a successful project, or executing the perfect jump shot on the basketball court, we sometimes find that the efforts we view as extraordinary and memorable go unnoticed or underappreciated by others. The same is true of the actions we wish to disown because they reflect poorly on our ability or character. They too may have less impact on our audience than we might think. An "obvious" social gaffe on a first date, an awkward stumble at the front of a line, or the misreading of a crucial passage of a prepared speech— each may seem shameful and unforgettable to us, but they often pass without notice by others.[3]

The spotlight effect causes us to have a distorted perspective of our own significance to the people around us, leading us to misjudge situations and make decisions based on our overly exaggerated feelings of visibility.

People Are Like Me

Fueling the spotlight effect is our tendency to overestimate how much others share our beliefs, opinions, habits, or preferences, another egocentric bias dubbed the "false consensus effect."[4] Because we are focused on what we are thinking, we tend to believe that the way we think is the norm for other people, too. We project our thinking onto others and end up believing there is more agreement for what we say, think, and do than is really the case. Furthermore, we think the world around us is judging us the same way we judge ourselves.

Reinforcing the belief is our tendency to associate with people who share our attitudes and opinions. Selective exposure. We use our social contacts to assess how common the characteristics are in the wider population. When we look around us to see what's "normal," our feedback is coming from a biased sample. The consequence is that most people believe that what they think and do is more commonplace than it really is.

Hard to Move an Anchor

The spotlight effect is an example of a phenomenon called "anchoring and adjustment."[5] Originally coined by Amos Tversky and Daniel Kahneman, anchoring describes how people tend to rely on the initial piece of information they receive to make subsequent judgments. They anchor to it. In this instance, the information early in the process is their own subjective experience that the spotlight is on them. Their attention is on a shirt they believe is socially embarrassing. People recognize that not everyone will be as focused on their shirt as they are—and they adjust—but they have difficulty adjusting far enough away from the anchor to accurately estimate how much attention other people are paying them.

The truth is that people are not focused on you like you are focused on yourself. They, like you, are more focused on themselves. They are wondering if *their* hair is out of place. They are wondering if *you* judged them for walking in late to the meeting. They are wondering if *you* admired the brilliant insight they offered on your team call. They, too, are at the center of their own universe.

Unless you are a Kardashian, you are likely not being watched, judged, and scrutinized nearly as much as you imagine.

When the Spotlight Is Actually on You

Of course, there are times when the spotlight is actually on you. *You are making a creative presentation to land the big account. You are sitting across the table from the company leaders for your fifth, and final, interview for your dream job. You're rolling out a new strategy for the board of directors.*

We all have moments that feel like our personal Super Bowl or World Cup, where the stakes seem higher than usual. I'm often asked, from a performance standpoint, are we better off treating these times under the spotlight as The Big Moment or just another moment?

My response? Either framework is valid. You just need to make a fundamental decision about which framework feels true to you and gives you the best chance for success.

Equally important—and the piece that often gets missed— is that a bespoke psychological-skills training program needs to be put in place ahead of time, regardless of which approach you take. The advantage of developing mental skills is that your internal experience is not dictated by your external environment.

If your first principle is "this is just another moment," then you develop the psychological practices to reinforce that. Start by identifying your ideal mindset, being clear on the most effective way to speak to yourself (self-talk), and dialing in the right level of focus and the optimal level of arousal inside your body. The goal is to be in a position where you have full command of yourself. Once you establish an ideal mindset, work to refine and develop command over it by continually practicing to achieve the ideal. You can use the ideal mindset as a reference point and target during mental training. Not confined to any particular environment, every moment of life becomes an opportunity to develop one's mental skills.

If you make the decision to treat that event as "the biggest moment of your life," you train the mental skills but you also intentionally create stressful scenarios to get closer to what that moment will be. Moments of high consequences and stress are created, played out, and replayed. Wrenches are continually thrown into the performance path. The practice is to calm the mind while the body is in an elevated state of agitation. If you do this over time, you get comfortable at higher levels of stress activation.

We can't always be in control of what comes at us in life, but we can control our response.

From Idea to Action

Turn down the light.

Simply recognizing that most people, to varying degrees, are moving through the world under their own spotlight—and are not focused on you—can help override your emotional programming and counteract the spotlight effect. The moment you internalize this concept, your relationship with FOPO will change.

Ask yourself whether you spend more time judging other people or thinking about how you are being perceived by other people. Most likely, you are busier with your own world, and for other people, it's the same. People often don't notice or care about things we are highly conscious of ourselves. They have work, family, kids, school, health challenges. You are nearly irrelevant to most people, especially to strangers. If someone does judge you or gives you a look, remember: they don't know you. They have their own stuff going on.

As an exercise, flip the script and think how you would feel being on the other side of the experience. First, pick an area where FOPO has surfaced for you. You were self-conscious of your age in a room full of younger or older people. You spoke up on a group call, but you never landed your point. You were overcome by a need to shoehorn your past successes into a conversation where they had no place and, after a momentary pause, someone lobbed you a follow-up question out of politeness, not awe. Next, consider when you have seem someone else act in a similar manner. Put that person in the spotlight of that moment and place yourself in the position of the listener or observer. Are you even thinking about that person's age? If so, was it just a passing thought? When the other person lost the thread of what he was saying, did you really care? Did you have a strong judgment about the person who flexed about a recent success or was what they shared somewhat interesting? Or did you shrug it off as relatable human behavior? You probably would not give those moments a second thought. They would likely seem unremarkable. Even forgettable. Self-conscious gaffes or socially witnessed stumbles fall into the category of things you said and things you did. For the most part, they are not moments felt and remembered by others.

Most people are too absorbed in their own lives to pay constant attention to the actions and behaviors of others. That glare is not someone shining a spotlight on you. You are shining the spotlight on yourself. Time to turn it down.

8

Do We Really Know What Someone Else Is Thinking?

There is nothing more deceptive than an obvious fact.

—ARTHUR CONAN DOYLE

I first started thinking about FOPO in graduate school. I was on a path toward a degree in psychology with a specialization in sport. I wanted to understand not what held people back but the qualities that enabled them to excel.

I was interested in how the best performers in the world organize their inner lives to perform in high-stakes environments. How was Charles Lindbergh able to fly alone, without a radio or parachute and sometimes just twenty feet above the waves, for thirty-four hours across the Atlantic Ocean? What enabled Jane Goodall to defy gender norms, navigate a realm of unknowns, and redefine the relationship between humans and animals? How did Ernest Shackleton and his crew on the

Endurance survive almost two years in a harrowing attempt to reach the South Pole?

I loved my area of study, but the stigma of traditional psychology seemed to hang over the field. Less than a century removed from locking people up for "madness," our culture still held overly negative beliefs about mental health. Going to a psychologist was widely seen as a sign of moral or character weakness. The perception was that psychology was about fixing poor mental health, not improving performance, investing in well-being, or flourishing. The rules that had been passed down from traditional psychology contributed to misperceptions about our field. Psychology was something that was supposed to be hidden from view. A client goes into a quiet sanctum and shares his or her inner world with a professional who vows never to publicly acknowledge the meeting or relationship. If a client runs into the psychologist outside the office, the psychologist is supposed to pass like a wordless ghost unless acknowledged by the client. It was like *Fight Club*: the first rule of psychology—don't talk about psychology. The secrecy that enveloped the business was an unintended recipe for shame.

The industry had written and unwritten rules, conventions, and practices that were held in place by people, laws, and a governing body. I was supposed to paint between the lines. I wanted to change that, to celebrate psychology and bring it out of the shadows. But I was afraid what others in my field would think if I went against the established way of doing things. So I moved to the edges of sports psychology after graduation. I began working in action and adventure sports (popularly known as extreme sports), a frontier where it seemed like the rules were still being written.

I had the fortune of being invited to work alongside one of the top mixed martial arts (MMA) fighters. After a five-month camp, we had our last training session and the team jumped on a flight to Las Vegas. We arrived three days before the event for weigh-ins, media interviews, and some on-premises training.

On the night of the competition, the fighter, his trainer, and I were in the dressing room going through the full preperformance routine: a physical warm-up, a technical warm-up, and a mindset warm-up. With the latter, the fighter gets his mind right, anchoring to his purpose, and "switching on" his ideal competitive mindset before entering the arena.

The walk to the cage can undo a fighter. The spotlight is on. The music is blaring. The roar of the crowd makes the hair on the back of your neck stand up. Nearly twenty thousand people in the stadium wanting to see blood (with millions at home tuning in for the same reason). The fighters are stepping into a high-conflict moment, a literal battleground, and the energy of the crowd is frenetic. Prefight anxiety is not uncommon, despite the confidence and bravado the fighters project. Getting into a steel cage with one of the most skilled fighters on the planet whose aim is to violently force you to quit fighting can rattle the nerves.

For world-class athletes, the details matter. We not only rehearsed the walk three times when the arena was empty; we had created mental imagery of the walk in the months leading up to the fight. To use imagery, an athlete activates all five senses to practice how he or she wants to feel and perform. This includes not only what happens in the cage, but the moments before those moments. How he wants to feel during warm-up in the ready room. How he wants to feel when joined by the camera crew and security guards as they wait for the green light to leave the room and step into the arena. How he wants to hold himself as he hears the chanting, screaming, booing, and cheering as he enters the arena.

Our team had prepared for this moment. We even practiced the hugs and handshakes before he walked up the steps to get into the cage. What we didn't practice is where the coaches go after those hugs.

On the evening of the fight, the walk up went exactly as planned. When we reached the octagon, we parted ways with the fighter, and the technical coordinator of the event directed us to our coaches' chairs, cutting across the sight line of the cameras.

When the bell rang, the fighter adhered to the game plan he had repeatedly visualized. He had little or no unnecessary movement, preserving his energy. He kept switching up his striking, so his more experienced opponent couldn't pick up any discernible pattern in his movements. He remained pre-ternaturally calm in the face of his opponent's increasing emotional engagement. He announced his arrival in style by taking down the overwhelming favorite. Our team was thrilled.

Months of hard work had paid off. I had veered off the beaten path for sports psychologists when I went to work in the MMA world. It turned out to be an incredible laboratory to understand how the mind works under pressure. There's very little margin for error in a hostile environment where a performer's mental skills—calm, confidence, focus, awareness—have to be razor sharp or the fighter pays an enormous price. I was quietly celebrating on the car ride home from the fight when my mentor called. The first words out of his mouth were "Gervais, what were you doing walking behind the athlete on television?"

His words hit me like a bus and confirmed my worst fears. He was well respected, a revered figure in our industry, and he was letting me know that psychology belonged behind closed doors. I was embarrassed that he thought I was doing something unbecoming for the field. In a nanosecond, the celebration ground to a halt and I wanted to crawl into a hole.

I called Lisa when I got back to the hotel to calibrate. Lisa is my high school sweetheart and we had been married for 10 years. She is Cuban and El Salvadorian by heritage, very blunt—a truth teller—and always my first stop when I need a reality check. She responded with two words, "Fuuuck him."

The Shift

Her counsel helped pull me out of my tailspin, but my mentor's opinion lingered for years. I made a point to steer clear of media for the better part of a decade. I did not want to be cast as self-aggrandizing.

Gradually, the media became increasingly interested in the mind and all its storytelling possibilities. It made sense. At the elite levels of sports, the game is played above the shoulders. The paper-thin margins between victory and defeat are more often than not determined by how skilled an athlete is at using their mind. The body is only an extension of what someone is capable of doing mentally.

I worked on a few projects that caught the media's attention and I was reminded of how much public conversations serve to destigmatize and promote psychology. I supported Austrian skydiver Felix Baumgartner in the Red Bull Stratos project when he jumped out of a pressurized capsule twenty-four miles above the earth's surface with a parachute strapped to his back and became the first human body to break the sound barrier without mechanized assistance.

I started working with the Seattle Seahawks as the first psychologist fully embedded in the organization and on the sidelines of the NFL. For nine years, I helped Coach Pete Carroll shape a relationship-based culture and make training the mind part of the DNA of the organization.

Kerri Walsh Jennings and Misty May-Treanor publicly talked about our mindset training work as they became the first beach volleyball players to win gold in three consecutive Olympic Games.

Later, I fired up the *Finding Mastery* podcast to put psychology on full display. Each week, I explore the psychological framework and mental skills of people on the path toward mastery.

I found a tremendous amount of support from colleagues for pulling back the curtain on psychology. For sure, there were industry custodians who were committed to business as usual, but I realized that much of my fear had been projected onto others. The truth was that I had my own internal monologue and judgments about pushing against convention. Who was I to challenge the wisdom of those who came before me?

I had vowed years earlier that if I ever ran into my mentor, I would find out the truth about his post-fight comments. I had assigned his opinion an enormous amount of meaning and importance. To me, he was the voice of psychological authority. He was the one carrying the stone tablet down the mountain. What exactly had he meant? Was his intention to put me in my place? Did he really see himself as the watchdog for tradition in psychology? Was he embarrassed I wasn't playing by the rules? Did he think I had overstepped my boundaries? Was he projecting his inner conflict onto me?

Then it happened. The moment. I had just finished speaking at a highly respected conference. I was walking away from the podium and I saw him sitting off to the side in the front row. Alone. We made eye contact. I thought to myself, *This is going to be my opportunity to understand exactly what he meant and why he said that years ago.* In the meet and greet after the event, we made eye contact again, but he was content sitting where he was. It struck me: *He wants me to walk over to him.* Finally, the crowd cleared. As I moved toward him, he looked smaller than I had remembered him. Almost frail. He was bearded, bespectacled, and wearing a herringbone tweed jacket—like he had been cast in the role of nineteenth-century psychologist.

By the time we were standing face to face, all the anxiousness I had about his opinion from years earlier dissipated. In that moment, I no longer cared. It seemed ridiculous that I had carried it with me for so long. We talked for a couple of minutes about the challenges facing the psychology business, shook hands, and moved on.

I had spent all those years carrying around his perceived opinion about me. It shaped career choices that I made or didn't make, opportunities that I seized or let pass by. For what? For an opinion that may not have been his opinion at all.

Defend or Explore?

My mentor's opinion more than a decade earlier seemed very clear at the time. *Gervais, the practice of psychology is private and belongs behind closed doors. You are breaking the unwritten rules. Know your place.*

I'll never really know what he was thinking, and it doesn't matter. What mattered was what I did with it. I didn't have the ability to be curious about what he said. I *knew* what he said. I was *certain* that I knew what he meant. His words just went through me like an electrical current. I reacted. I didn't defend myself, but I took a defensive position. I protected myself by playing it small, playing it safe, vowing not to expose myself to that kind of criticism again.

After our handshake, I began to examine why his response had had such an impact on me. Why did his opinion matter so much? Why did I let an external event dictate my internal experience? What could it teach me about my own inner world?

Since my early days of graduate school, I had been straddling the line between the path I wanted to pursue and the path that I was supposed to follow, full of signposts, rules, and traditions. I couldn't figure out how to square that circle. It was like a Zen koan: How can one play by the rules and break them at the same time?

My mentor's response triggered something I had been carrying for a long time. I had a fear about what other people would think if I went against the grain in the field of psychology. I had a powerful internal narrative going on about what "they"—a hazily defined group of people who wielded power in my chosen field—would say if I didn't stay in my lane.

I could hear Einstein's quote running on a loop in my head, "A question that sometimes drives me hazy: Am I or are the others crazy?" When my mentor opened his mouth after the fight, his words spilled out, but I infused them with meaning, weight, and my own interpretation. His admonishment for being in the background as the fighter entered the ring threw fuel on a charged belief that I already held.

He stepped right into the middle of a story that was already going on inside me.

A Distinctive Skill but Not a Superpower

Human beings have the unique cognitive capacity to think about their own mind and the mind of others. We are able to make inferences about other people's mental states—what they intend, think, feel, and believe—and use them to "understand and predict behavior." We do it throughout the day, almost reflexively, in every social interaction we have.

Our ability to discern what someone else might be thinking is a foundation of our social interactions—an important social skill that most people start developing in early childhood. Ziv Williams, MD, an associate professor of neurosurgery at Harvard Medical School, notes, "When we interact, we must be able to form predictions about another person's unstated intentions and thoughts. This ability requires us to paint a mental picture of someone's beliefs, which involves acknowledging that those beliefs may be different from our own and assessing whether they are true or false."[1]

We are all mind readers, some better than others, but are we very good at discerning what's in the minds of other people?[2]

University of Chicago professor Nicholas Epley, PhD, and his colleagues organized a simple experiment to find out.

Epley separated romantic couples into different rooms. One partner was given a series of twenty statements and opinions with which he or she had to agree or disagree, ranging on a scale from 1 (strongly disagree) to 7 (strongly agree).[3] The statements were things like "If I had to live my life over, I would sure do things differently," and "I would like to spend a year in London or Paris," and "I would rather spend a quiet evening at home than go out to a party." In the adjoining room, the other partner predicted how their partner would answer each question. That person also had to estimate the number of questions they believe they correctly predicted.

The couples had been together for an average of 10.3 years, which drifts into that relationship stage where sentence finishing kicks into high gear. Fifty-eight percent were married. Presumably, partners would be able to read the minds of their partners better than they would read the minds of strangers. If not, it could make for a long car ride home.

As imagined, the partners' ability to infer their spouse's thoughts and feelings was better than random guessing—but not by much. Random guessing would enable someone to correctly predict 2.85 answers, whereas the partners answered 4.9 of the 20 questions correctly.

More revealing than the accuracy of their mind reading was the chasm between their perceived ability to accurately discern their partner's thoughts and their actual ability. Although they had correctly answered, on average, 4.9 of the questions, they believed they correctly predicted 12.6 out of the 20 questions. In other words, we think we are much better at knowing what's going on inside someone's head than we actually are. In Epley's words, "The problem is that the confidence we have in this sense far outstrips our actual ability, and the confidence we have in our judgment rarely gives us a good sense of how accurate we actually are."[4]

Epley's experiment showed how subpar our mind-reading abilities really are. And it's not like the people he tasked with guessing other people's thoughts were strangers. He recruited spouses—people who had spent years of their lives together. People who knew the intimate details of each other's lives.

If we're so bad at predicting what those closest to us are thinking, imagine how bad we are at predicting what our friends, bosses, colleagues, mentors, and strangers think about us.

The point is, we spend a lot of time and mental resources obsessing about things that we're most likely wrong about. As someone who works with high performers, I can say that I've never come across a high-performing mind reader. In fact, we're all bad at it.

The all-too-common belief that we *know* what someone is thinking, and what they are thinking about us, is often the match that lights the FOPO fire. We preemptively act, or react, to our own thoughts that may or may not be true. We are certain we know how someone feels about us, but unless they actually express what they are thinking, our "knowing" is just speculation. More often than not, we are just stringing together our thoughts into a story that makes sense of the world in that moment. It's simply our interpretation of that experience. And that interaction is most often misguided, skewed, or flat-out wrong. In the words of Nobel Prize–winning psychologist Daniel Kahneman, "We're generally overconfident in our opinions and our impressions and judgments. We exaggerate how knowable the world is."[5]

Ask Rather Than Intuit

Or maybe we just need to step into someone's proverbial shoes to understand what goes on in their mind. Epley led a series of experiments with Mary Steffel, PhD, and Tal Eyal to see if actively taking the perspective of another person enables us to predict their thoughts, feelings, attitudes, or other mental states more accurately.[6] Dale Carnegie encouraged readers in that direction in his classic motivational guide from 1935, *How to Win Friends and Influence People*.[7] His eighth principle is "Try honestly to see things from the other person's point of view." It seems like common sense that if we imagine, honestly, another person's psychological point of view, we'll have a better sense of what goes on in their minds.

Well, not exactly.

Results from their experiments found no evidence that actively considering another person's perspective systematically increased the ability to read someone else's mind. "If anything, perspective taking decreased accuracy overall while occasionally increasing confidence in judgment."[8]

What gets in the way of our ability to discern what's in the mind of another person? What prevents us from truly knowing their opinions and intuiting the intention and meaning behind their words? We are attempting to decode the most complicated and adaptive system in the universe. We have an estimated 86 billion neurons in the human brain. Each neuron can be directly connected to roughly one thousand to ten thousand other neurons through synapses, according to V. S. Ramachandran, a neuroscientist and the director of the Center for Brain and Cognition at the University of California, San Diego.[9]

Given the complexity of the human mind, there's one strategy Eyal, Steffel, and Epley's study found valuable in understanding what goes on in the mind of another person.

Inquiry.

Rather than taking the perspective of another person, ask them. The most accurate insight into the thoughts, words, beliefs, and opinions of someone else comes from asking them to describe what's "going on in their minds in a context where they can report it both honestly and accurately."[10]

If you are wondering about someone's opinion, stop guessing, ask directly and listen.

I would have benefited from that insight years earlier with my mentor. If I had asked him directly about his opinion years earlier, rather than assuming my interpretation to be true, I would have benefited. I wouldn't have necessarily gotten to the truth of his experience but I may have better understood the truth of my own. How we interpret someone's opinion often reflects more about ourselves than the person who expressed the opinion. But we don't realize it. Our interpretation becomes the "truth" and we lose our ability to be curious about it. We get swept up in our narrative and focus on the antagonist of the story rather than ourselves.

By asking my mentor directly, I would've gained a more complete and accurate understanding of his thoughts and feelings. It might have left open the possibility of not just having a relationship with him, but a deeper relationship than we had up to that point. Maybe if I had dug down, I would have discovered that he actually shared my desire to destigmatize and remove the shame around psychology. Who knows? Anything is possible. What is certain, though, is that my response (disconnection) foreclosed any possibility of having a relationship with him.

Perhaps more significantly, I would have reached a deeper understanding of my own self by engaging him. Rather than moving from my feelings and placing my attention on his, it would have been an opportunity to tease apart, hold up in the light, and express my own complicated feelings about the career I was about to embark on. The simple act of bringing ourselves forward is an antidote to FOPO because FOPO is fueled by passivity and projection.

People's opinions only have power over us to the degree that we give them that power. On that night in Las Vegas long ago, I gave my mentor's opinion too much power. There was a different path I could have taken—and it started with simple inquiry.

From Idea to Action

If you want to test your mind-reading skills, try this. Ask a partner, friend, or a supervisor if you really want to stir the pot, if you can take a few moments to try to read their mind.

Grab a pad of paper and a pen, and let's dive into the fascinating realm of mind reading. Here's how it works:

1. Set the stage: find a comfortable space and place an object between the two of you. It could be anything— a cell phone, a candle, a set of keys—just a simple, everyday item that really serves as a stimulus to misdirect their attention. If you are going to play the role, you may as well go all in.

2. Choose your mind-reading style: decide how you prefer to tap into your mind-reading powers. You can choose to close your eyes and immerse yourself in a deep state of concentration, or keep your eyes open, observing the subtle cues and expressions of the other person. Find what works best for you.

3. The thought and the impression: ask the other person to focus on a specific thought and write it down on the paper. It can be anything that comes to mind—words, images, or even a memory. Encourage them to explore the depths of their imagination. Next, request that they form an opinion or idea about you and write it down as well. This will challenge your mind-reading abilities on a personal level.

4. Unleash your mind reading: now comes the moment to showcase your mind-reading prowess. Share with the other person what you believe their initial thought was and the opinion they formed about you. Express your insights and perceptions with clarity and conviction.

5. Compare: finally, compare your perceptions to what was actually going on in their mind. How did you do unlocking

the secrets hidden within the minds of others? Are you ready to quit your day job and hang your own shingle?

We all, to varying degrees, try to mind read. We continually try to discern what other people are thinking. We scrutinize words, tone, facial expressions, postures, actions, and choices for clues. To heighten the challenge, people are aware this activity is happening in the background and try to control or guide the perceptions we are forming. An unspoken game of concealment, discovery, and mistaken revelation.[11]

The ability to think about the mind of another is part of what makes us deeply social animals. But are we good at it? Not particularly. Certainly not to the point that we should be shaping life decisions and strategies around what we intuit to be in the mind of another human being. Just ask.

9

We See Things as ~~They~~ We Are

What the human being is best at doing is interpreting all new information so that their prior conclusions remain intact.

—WARREN BUFFETT

In 2015, Cecilia Bleasdale went shopping in a small village in Lancashire, England, for a dress for her daughter's wedding. She snapped a photo of her £50 purchase, and two other dresses she had considered, and sent the photos to her daughter. Her daughter responded by asking if she bought the "white and gold one." No, her mom replied, "it's blue and black." "Mum," said her daughter, "if you think that's blue and black you need to go and see the doctor."[1]

Her daughter shared the photo on Facebook. Two weeks later the wedding went off without a hitch in Scotland and little attention was paid to Cecilia's dress. But a friend of her daughter's, Caitlin McNeill, couldn't get the photo out of her head and posted it in on Tumblr, asking for help identifying the color of the dress. The next day the internet exploded with interest and the post went viral. Kanye West, Kim Kardashian, and Taylor Swift all weighed in on the debate. A tech team had to be brought in to prevent Buzzfeed's servers from crashing.[2] Cecilia landed on the *Ellen DeGeneres Show*. The dress became the topic of a global conversation, including inside the science community. Why was the world seeing the dress in two dramatically different ways?

Perception Is Not Passive

Neuroscience ultimately supplied the answer: perception is idiosyncratic.

A person's conclusion about the color of the dress depends on the *assumption* their brain makes about the ambient light and how the dress was illuminated.[3] We cannot tell from the photo whether the dress sits in a shadow against a brightly lit background or whether the entire room is brightly lit and the colors are washed out. In the absence of facts, our brain makes hypotheses and inferences to fill in the gaps. What we perceive as our conscious reality is the conclusion of those inferences. Our conclusion is based on an assumption. A belief.

The principle extends beyond visual perception.

We tend to think of perception as taking in sensory information and piecing together what we are trying to perceive. That's called bottom-up processing. We start with no preconceived idea of what we are looking at and make sense of the information received by our senses. Perception then directs our cognitive understanding. For example, imagine you were given a jigsaw puzzle without the cover of the box to show you what the completed puzzle looks like.[4] You look at each piece and then begin to put the pieces together and gradually a recognizable image starts to take shape.

In actuality, the brain doesn't just passively perceive reality. It creates reality through the filter of our beliefs. We use context, previous experiences, knowledge, and expectation to interpret new information.

Starting when we are young, the brain builds a simulated picture or model of the world that it has to navigate.[5] Not a big fan of the unexpected, the brain predicts what is going to happen based on our mental models. Those predictions become critical filters for our experience of the world around us. Rather than information bubbling up, the top-down predictive process is a filter that shapes our immediate experience. We experience our lives, much like we experience Cecilia Bleasdale's dress, through an interpretive process based on the beliefs embedded in our mental model of the world.

Perception is a constructive process, and our constructions are often misrepresentations of reality. We see things, like Cecilia Bleasdale's dress, other than they are. We fail to see the gorilla who walks through a group of basketball players in Daniel Simons's famous experiment about inattentional blindness.[6] We see the moon larger on the horizon than when it's high in the sky even though it's the same size. Often we "perceive only what we expect to perceive rather than what is there." As York University psychology professor James Alcock writes, "Our thoughts and feelings, our actions and reactions, respond not to the world as it actually is—for we never know reality directly—but to the world as we believe it to be."[7]

The Filters

Similarly, how we perceive and interpret other people's opinions is wholly dependent upon our beliefs and biases. To paraphrase Alcock, in most cases we are not reacting and responding to the opinions of others as they actually are because we don't know the mind of another human being; rather, we are responding to their opinions as we believe them to be. Our beliefs act as filters through which we interpret the opinions of others.

To understand the role our beliefs play in fueling FOPO, it's important to recognize that FOPO is a *preemptive* process. In an effort to increase relational acceptance and avoid rejection, we try to anticipate what someone is thinking about us. We are continually gauging our social environment for information that signals either threat or opportunity. The whole goal is to maximize acceptance and avoid being ridiculed, laughed at, mistreated, bullied, singled out, or ostracized. In our hypervigilance, we scan to pick up microclues, so we can preemptively embrace, change, or reject the opinion. Our anxiousness is fueled by the not knowing. As Alfred Hitchcock said, "There's no terror in the bang, only in the anticipation of it."

We want to prevent something (an unfavorable opinion) that has not yet occurred (and may not be happening at all) but presents a potential threat. Unsure about the other person's intent, we rely on our own interpretation of what they are thinking about us. Our interpretation is backed by the belief system we hold about ourselves and human nature. Under threat, we tend to anchor even more strongly to our beliefs. We often scan our environment for evidence that matches up with what we already know to discern what's in the mind of another person.

What we perceive to be true about someone's opinion and what's actually true are not always the same. Our interpretation of the opinions of others often reflects more about what's inside us, and our own beliefs, than the opinion of the other person. When we act on what we believe will happen before it actually happens, we are actually helping create the experience, a psychological phenomenon known as the interpersonal expectancy effect.

That's not some kind of metaphysical notion. It's how the human mind and brain work. Let's say you had a good friend who stood by you through a difficult time in your life. He demonstrated incredible generosity and thoughtfulness during a time when you felt really vulnerable. A few years later, he goes through a relationship upheaval. You are swept up in work, still on your heels from your own challenges. He's not the type to reach out in need. He's well-loved and has a lot of support. You see him less frequently. After a period of time, you have a gnawing feeling that he thinks you did not show up for him. You have no evidence for your thesis, but you back away from the friendship. You feel more self-conscious. The spontaneity and freedom you had to drop by his house are no longer there. Years go by and slowly the void grows.

In this instance, you created the narrative and took steps (pulling back, not stopping by his home) consistent with the outcome you predicted.

Confirmation Bias

The human mind tends to look for, interpret, and remember information in a way that affirms our existing beliefs or expectations, a term coined "confirmation bias" in 1970 by English psychologist Peter Wason. In a series of studies, he found that people preferred to find information that confirmed what they already held to be true. They would overlook or ignore the information that did not conform to their beliefs.[8] Confirmation bias primarily happens outside conscious awareness so people are generally unaware of the source and impact of their biases.[9]

When I first studied confirmation bias, I started seeing it everywhere. Sorry, that's a grad school joke, but it sort of hints at the idea. We often find evidence that supports a belief we already have rather than looking for evidence that challenges that belief.

Confirmation bias has long been thought to impact thought and behavior. Renaissance philosopher Sir Francis Bacon, who popularized scientific methodology, recognized it more than four hundred years ago:

> The human understanding when it has once adopted an opinion (either as being the received opinion or as being agreeable to itself) draws all things else to support and agree with it. And though there be a greater number and weight of instances to be found on the other side, yet these it either neglects and despises, or else by some distinction sets aside and rejects; in order that by

this great and pernicious predetermination the authority of its former conclusions may remain inviolate.[10]

Daniel Kahneman, one of the most influential psychologists in the past fifty years, argues that we think much like we see: "In visual perception you have a process that suppresses ambiguity, so a single interpretation is chosen and you are not aware of the ambiguity."[11] Consider the ambiguous duck-rabbit illusion, first made famous by American psychologist Joseph Jastrow (see figure 9-1). People viewing the image cannot see one figure as a duck and the other as a rabbit even though their features are spatially distinct. Our brain switches between seeing a rabbit or a duck. We can't hold both images in our brain at the same time.

"Confirmation bias comes from when you have an interpretation, and you adopt it, and then, top down, you force

FIGURE 9-1

Duck-rabbit illusion

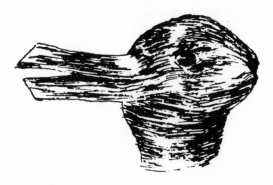

Source: Creative Commons

everything to fit that interpretation," Kahneman says. "That's a process that we know occurs in perception that resolves ambiguity, and it's highly plausible that a similar process occurs in thinking."[12]

The bias is partly born out of our brain's need to find the most efficient way to consolidate the vast amount of information that pours in, a process called heuristics. Heuristics generate deeply grooved neurological channels that opt for speed and efficiency at the expense of accuracy, the familiar over the unfamiliar.

For much of our evolutionary history, we needed to be highly attuned to threats to our physical survival. If you heard a snapping of a twig, leaping to the conclusion that it was tiger in the woods could save your life. In the modern world, these mental shortcuts can be useful when we don't have the luxury of making judgments supported by clear and copious data. But they can also lead us astray.

To illustrate, I worked with an executive at a startup tech company. His relationship with work created intense impairment in other areas of his life. He lives by the credo that success comes from hard work and long hours. The company's sales had slumped in the previous two quarters. Searching for an explanation, he concluded the downturn was a result of complacency and the sales team putting in fewer hours.

He had evidence for his thesis. Though he had less direct oversight of employees under the company's hybrid work model, he knew his sales team was working fewer hours during the regular workday as they openly balanced the demands that came with working from home. He decided to bring everyone back to the office and end the work-from-home experiment. But sales didn't improve. Costs rose. He lost two of his top salespeople, who didn't want to return to the office. Employee morale and mental health slumped as the quick return stirred up anxiety.

The company brought in a management consultant to better understand the constriction of the business. Able to have an honest dialogue with the employees, the consultant quickly recognized that complacency was not the issue. The CEO heavily weighted the confirming evidence (fewer hours during the workday), but he failed to recognize that his remote employees were actually working more total hours because of the time spent digitally connected on weekends and after normal business hours. The issue was burnout. The employees were emotionally, physically, and mentally exhausted by the demands of their always-on, 24-7 work culture. His bias not only left the CEO unattuned to the employees' well-being; it actually exacerbated the underlying problem.

Beyond Belief

Beliefs are thoughts or ideas we hold to be true. Our beliefs winnow down a limitless world into a particular perceptual experience of reality. We go to war for our beliefs. We go to jail for our beliefs. We walk down the aisle for our beliefs. Some beliefs empower us and others constrain us. Ultimately, all beliefs are limiting, even the empowering ones. They limit us by defining us.

We are faced with a choice every time we perceive that someone has an opinion about us that may present a threat. Are we going to validate our belief system, which can set us down the path of FOPO, or will we choose to be curious? Are we going to interpret this moment through the lens of our past experiences, or are we going to experience it like we have never seen it before? Because we haven't. This is a brand-new moment.

We All Have Biases

We all have biases, preferences, or aversions to different people, things, or ideas—some that we are unable to recognize. If you don't think that's the case, ask yourself how you feel about people who:

- Support the National Rifle Association (NRA)

- Believe female transgender athletes should be able to compete in athletic competitions

- Think elementary school children should not have to stand for the pledge of allegiance

- Call climate change a hoax

- Say the solution to the homeless problem is government housing in your neighborhood

- Want to mandate vaccines

- Drive an electric car

- Prefer cats over dogs

Some beliefs or feelings might have been stirred up as you read through the list. Our brain naturally catalogs things into categories and groups, likes and dislikes.

From Idea to Action

To better understand how confirmation bias shapes your interpretation of other people's opinions, proactively seek information that challenges your beliefs. Your task is to revisit your interpretation of someone's perceived opinion of you. It could be an opinion that was directly expressed or something that wasn't verbally expressed but you picked up on. For example, *My supervisor feels threatened by me so she's not pulling me onto the team for the new account. She's an old-school, top-down manager who values control more than empowering people.*

Break it into two parts: your belief and their opinion. Start with your belief. *My supervisor feels threatened by me and wants to be in control.* Chances are this is not the first time you've entertained this belief. You have something in your history that supports it. Consider whether there are other experiences that may have informed your perception of your boss. Jot down your evidence for the belief. The evidence could be very broad and generalized. *All companies want top-down control.* It could be an experience you had at a previous company. *My manager never had my back. It was always about him.* It might be a specific experience with your boss. *She rolled her eyes when I talked about my enthusiasm for the company's new account.* Or it might be all the above.

Whatever the evidence may be, recognize that that's the filter through which you interpreted the opinion.

Now flip over to the other person's opinion. In the example, she does not want you on the team. Play with some other interpretations of why you weren't pulled onto the account. Even if you don't think it's true, entertain it. Indulge the idea. Use your imagination to the point it might feel like a creative writing exercise. *My supervisor really values me, but her hands were tied on this account because of a prior obligation to another executive. She wants to put me in a situation where I can really flourish. She rolled her eyes because she was frustrated by her inability to bring me on the team.*

The mission is to try to understand the experience from an alternative point of view and to uncouple, even briefly, from the confirming biases you already hold that may shape your perception of someone else's opinion about you.

10

Social Beings Masquerading as Separate Selves

No man is an island, entire of itself;
every man is a piece of the continent,
a part of the main.

—JOHN DONNE

In the winter following the 1998 baseball season, superstar Barry Bonds caught up with his longtime friend and fellow star, Ken Griffey Jr., for dinner at Griffey's home in Florida. In the previous season, Bonds had seen Mark McGwire destroy Major League Baseball's home run record with, as it was later confirmed, the help of steroids.

At the table, Bonds expressed his frustration that the playing field wasn't level, and he made a surprising admission: "I had a helluva season last year, and nobody gave a crap. Nobody. As much as I've complained about McGwire and Canseco and all of the bull with steroids, I'm tired of fighting it. I turn 35 this year. I've got three or four good seasons left, and I wanna get paid. I'm just gonna start using some hard-core stuff, and hopefully it won't hurt my body. Then I'll get out of the game and be done with it."[1]

Bonds found himself in what mathematician Albert Tucker called "the prisoner's dilemma."[2] The prisoner's dilemma was born out of the field of game theory, but for more than sixty years it has been used by psychologists, economists, political scientists, and evolutionary biologists to understand what drives human behavior. There are many variations of the prisoner's dilemma, but the basic construct is that two people who have never met play against each other. The outcome of the game is interdependent. The choices each person makes and how they play the game affect the outcome for them and the outcome for their opponent. The choice that each person makes is private, then revealed to one another once each person finalizes their decision. The dilemma is that the game can be played selfishly, as a zero-sum affair where you maximize the gain for yourself but at the expense of a smaller gain for the other person. Or the game can be played more cooperatively by maximizing the gain that you jointly earn, but at the expense of you getting less than if you had played selfishly.

In the case of Barry Bonds, he could have made the communal choice to not take performance-enhancing drugs. That would likely have resulted in reduced (short-term) rewards— less fame, statistical records, and money—but would have benefited the players who were playing by the rules.

Not surprisingly, and as economists would predict, the vast majority of people play the game selfishly. The results support the widely held belief, embedded in the Western world, that humans are driven by self-interest. That view has been reflected in hundreds of iterations of the game. It has also been the primary framework through which we understand economic and social behavior.

Through this lens, it's probably not surprising that Bonds found himself embroiled in a steroids scandal. He played the game selfishly. And, if you agree that we're a self-interested species, most of us would have done the same.

But that's not the whole story.

Varda Liberman, Steven M. Samuels, and Lee Ross led a study with another version of the game with the exact same premise, same rules, same everything—with one slight change. At the start of the game, the participants were told they would be playing the "community game."[3] The results were dramatically different. Seventy percent of the participants played cooperatively—with the larger group in mind—rather than selfishly.

The study demonstrated, and is now supported by a wide body of evidence across disciplines, that humans are not just selfishly driven but socially driven creatures. Our social drive is not something we learn, a pragmatic skill we acquire to support our narrow self-interest. As social neuroscientist Matthew Lieberman describes it, "Our social operating system is part of the basic components of who we are as mammals."[4]

We are not individuals who have learned to be social. We are social animals who have learned to identify as separate selves.

That's worth repeating.

We are fundamentally social. And truly understanding and reminding ourselves that we need true connection will help us work with FOPO.

In fact, FOPO is born out of a deep desire to be accepted and connected to others. It's a basic human need to belong. The fear of someone's negative opinion is a symptom of a deeper fear: being rejected. The deeply biologically ingrained consequence of rejection is what drives FOPO's pervasive nature. It might seem like the antidote to FOPO is to simply not care about what someone thinks of you.

In its simplest form, the solution—the antidote to FOPO—has two dimensions: (1) to have deep love and care for others' well-being and to be a contributor to the social fabric our biology is optimized for, and (2) to act in alignment with one's purpose, values, and goals. This in return promotes thoughts and actions that create a rising tide for both others and self. When we act in alignment with loving others and at the same time working toward one's purpose, there is very little space for the mental energy consumed by worrying about what others may or may not be thinking about you.

Missed Connection

When I was in sixth grade, my family and I were living in Northern California. One afternoon my mother asked, "Michael, is everything okay with you?"

She would often check in with me, but this time it felt different. I knew exactly what she was asking about. I paused for a moment and said, "No."

She waited. I looked away and did a quick calculus of what to do with the swelling behind my eyes and the tension building in my throat. I said again, "No, I'm not okay." I said it more to break the silence than anything else.

She picked up on the cadence, waited a few beats, and responded, "Okay, what's going on?"

I wanted to put her at ease and pass it off as a fleeting feeling, but I decided to say it. "I just feel like there's an empty hole inside me. Like I'm missing something. It's right here," pointing to my stomach and chest, "Like God's not there, nothing is there."

Still not making eye contact, she said, "Okay," and gently reached for my hand and pulled me in for a warm hug, gently wrapping one arm around my back and the other holding the back of my head. We stayed there for a bit longer than usual. Nothing else was said. In that moment, I was okay.

For years thereafter I felt that loneliness, an empty feeling that lived just below the surface. You'd never know it from the outside everything was "fine." And for the most part, I was fine. I did not examine that feeling much. I just kind of knew it was there. Not unrelatedly, I became proficient at entertaining three other emotions: excitement (chasing thrills via high-octane risk-based sports like surfing, skateboarding, and skiing), anxiousness (worrying about all the things that could go wrong later), and anger (quick to temper as a release mechanism to not have to feel anxiety or sadness). Looking back, the emptiness I felt wasn't depression or adolescent angst. It was an awareness that I wasn't connected the way I wanted to be connected—with myself, with others, and with nature.

Separate Self

The belief in our separateness, and the failure to recognize that we are part of a greater whole, has given rise to the uniquely modern phenomenon of the separate self.

For most of human history, the individual, and the needs and desires of the individual, were secondary to those of the larger group. In the early days of man, it was not possible for a member of the tribe to act solely in their self-interest. Sublimating personal desires in deference to the norms and values of the group was essential for survival. That's no longer the case in the modern world.

In the twenty-first century, the functional ties that bind us have loosened.

Immediate threats to our physical survival have been greatly diminished, and the need to rely on the group for protection has been correspondingly reduced. The "tribe" is not essential for immediate physical survival.

Technology has weakened physical connection. We spend more time staring at our phones than each other. We text rather than meet. Emojis substitute for physical cues like facial expressions and body language. "Likes" replace words of encouragement. "LOL" substitutes for the physical act of laughing. A "heart" serves as a stand-in for a warm embrace.

Geographic mobility allows us to hopscotch in and out of communities. We move in search of more favorable economic opportunities, better weather, or less expensive housing, while technology sustains the illusion of connectedness.

Culture of Self

We have put the self at the center of Western life in the twenty-first century and, in the process, we have untethered ourselves from the whole of who we are. The idolatry of the self has reached its apogee in human history. Never has the idea of a separate self occupied such a prominent place in society. The self has supplanted the group or community as the basic building block of society. Individual rights, needs, and wants are sacrosanct, and the individual is the filter through which we view economic, legal, and moral problems. The life of the self is an individual adventure. The goals of the self are individual happiness and self-realization. The question that's always out in front of the self is, What do I need to do to find *my* happiness?

On the surface, it looks like we may have fulfilled the observation that French philosopher and social scientist Alexis de Tocqueville made about America more than a century and a half ago when he wrote that most Americans "feel no longer bound to their fate by a common interest; each of them, standing aloof, thinks that he is reduced to care for himself alone."[5]

Uncoupling the self from a larger social context creates a host of conditions that fuel FOPO.

In the culture of self, both achievements and failures are perceived to depend entirely on one's own efforts. While that idea can be a source of motivation ("you can change the world"), it can also work against mental health. When we identify as a separate self, we take authorship of what happens around us, including those things we don't control. Life unfolds. Things happen. And then we layer on the subjective interpretation that they are happening to me. They are happening because of me, because of something I am doing or not doing. We give ourselves too much credit when things go well and too much blame when things don't work out. We often feel like we are not good enough, like something inside of us is unlikable. We turn our experiences against ourselves and they become a referendum on our self. Consequently, we are continually in pursuit of our worth and evading the fear of our inadequacy. We are running to stay ahead of our self-judgments and the opinions and judgments of others.

Impostor syndrome is an outgrowth of our self-driven culture, an unintentional rebellion against the self's instinct to point back at itself. People with impostor syndrome, often high achievers, tend to attribute success not to their own abilities but to luck or high effort. Unable to internalize the full body of their work, all their successes, mistakes, failures, and hard-earned insights, they fear the opinions of others will match the hidden opinion they hold of themselves.

The ever-present need to prove (or defend) our self distances us from others and undermines our relationships. As author Mark Manson puts it, "A person's ability to engage in a genuine connection is inversely proportional to their need to prove themselves."[6] The focus is on meeting the needs of oneself, not the other person or the relationship. In the process we often put ourselves in competition, rather than collaboration, with the other person. Rather than being a part of the circle of people we trust, we push them away, often into the realm of people's opinions we fear.

The self-help industry fuels our obsession with self. We focus on ourselves at the exclusion of everything and everyone around us. Surrounded by advice—books, articles, podcasts, blog posts, therapists, influencers—we insatiably search for that tip, trick, or hack that's going to heal our childhood trauma, or at least improve our match rate on Bumble. Therapy sessions drag on for months and years with no finish line in sight. We dive down the rabbit hole of our childhood so we can get an honest handle on our history. We relentlessly search inside ourselves for the key that will unlock our wholeness.

Putting self at the center of our world separates us from the planet we inhabit. When we place ourselves above the earth rather than on it, we deplete our resources, degrade our planet's habitats and put the globe in peril of overheating. Environmental journalist Richard Schiffman poetically describes our disconnection from the natural world: "At the core of our abuse of nature is the belief that we humans are essentially islands unto ourselves, alienated from the world beyond our skins. A little god locked within the gated community of his or her own skull won't feel much responsibility for what goes on outside."[7]

In our self-driven culture, meaning and purpose are conscripted by the individual. Each person is responsible for figuring out their unique purpose, rather than it being interpreted through the relationships we have with others, the broader society, and the planet. The question to ponder is: Are we independent people in opportunistic association with one another or does meaning spring from being in service to the relationship of the collective?

The Myth of Self-Reliance

The self-reliance myth that underpins our culture of self makes for great storytelling and effective branding but masks a fundamental truth: no one does it alone. I work with some of the greatest individual athletes, artists, and business leaders on the planet. To a person, there's a universal recognition that great feats require strong teams of people that lock arms with each other. The narrative about the lone genius—Steve Jobs, Charles Lindbergh, Mother Teresa, Harriet Tubman, Ferdinand Magellan, Vincent van Gogh—who alters the course of history through sheer inspiration, determination, and talent does not accurately reflect reality.

NYU Professor Scott Galloway points at the reality that hides behind the myth: "Persistence and the plow 'settled' the frontier, not a handsome white guy with a six-shooter and a pack of smokes. Cowboys were poor men who did dreary work for low wages; Hollywood and Madison Avenue morphed them into gunslinging heroes. Likewise, the wonders of Silicon Valley were built on a foundation of government-funded projects— the computer chip, the internet, the mouse, the web browser, and the GPS."[8]

Self-reliance and rugged individualism are embedded in the Western psyche, but there's a more foundational need: the human need to belong.

Belonging

In 1995, two leading social psychologists, Roy Baumeister and Mark Leary, published a landmark article suggesting that belonging is not just a desire but a need, a deeply rooted human motivation that shapes our thoughts, feelings, and behaviors.[9]

Up to that point, belonging had not really been considered as a motive behind human social behavior. Baumeister and Leary posited that the desire for social acceptance and belonging may be *the* motive that accounts for more human behavior than any other motive. *Why do we make ourselves attractive to others? Why are we nice to other people? Why do we get a hit of dopamine when someone presses the "like" button? Why do we contort to fit in? Why do we perseverate on how others might perceive us?*

Baumeister and Leary held that forming and maintaining bonds helped our ancestors survive and reproduce. A solitary human could not have survived on the African savanna six million years ago. We only survived because we formed groups. People in groups could gather, grow, and hunt for food, find mates, look after children, and better defend themselves.

Living in groups was only half the challenge. People had to first gain acceptance into the group. They had to get the others to want them as a group member. In Leary's words, "Accompanying our desire to affiliate and be in groups was a desire to get other people to accept us."

The need to belong has been wired into our brain for millions of years. Our social nature, however, goes deeper than merely gaining acceptance and belonging. It's in our nature to have as the center of one's life not "me" but "us."

Interconnected

The separate self is a made-up construct that leaves us cut off from the world around us and cut off from the world inside us. Not unlike what I felt when I was twelve years old, we sense that something is missing in our lives, but we cannot put a finger on it. A longing for connection. A sadness that our whole being is not seen. We experience ourselves as alone in the world. We have a pervasive, unsatiable craving to know that we matter, to know that we belong. We look outward for the answer. We look to others for confirmation that we are okay, that we are actually part of something larger than ourselves.

It doesn't matter, though, what other people say or do. They can tell you they love you. They can make you a part of the team. They can bring you into their organization. They can invite you to the party. They can acknowledge you in the company meeting. They can like your Instagram post. They can ask you to marry them. But they cannot make the longing go away that comes from believing you are a separate self, an island unto yourself. They cannot give you the feeling of connection you deeply desire. Only you can.

We look outside of ourselves for something that sits inside of us. We have disconnected from the fundamental truth that we are an inherently social species that is interconnected to everything and everyone around us. Our interdependence is an inexorable fact of life.[10]

We are intertwined on a functional level, but our relationship to each other is not just pragmatic. It's not just based on a need to be able to borrow a cup of sugar from the neighbor.

We are interdependent on a global level. As evolutionary biologist Lynn Margulis writes:

> Darwin's biggest contribution was to show us that all individual organisms are connected through time. It

doesn't matter whether you compare kangaroos, bacteria, humans, or salamanders, we all have incredible chemical similarities. . . . [The Russian geochemist Vladimir] Vernadsky showed us that organisms are not only connected through time but also through space. The carbon dioxide we exhale as a waste product becomes the life-giving force for a plant; in turn, the oxygen waste of a plant gives us life. . . . But the connection doesn't stop at the exchange of gases in the atmosphere. We are also physically connected, and you can see evidence of this everywhere you look. Think of the protists that live in the hindgut of the termite, or the fungi that live in the rootstock of trees and plants. The birds that flitter from tree to tree transport fungi spores throughout the environment. Their droppings host a community of insects and microorganisms. When rain falls on the droppings, spores are splashed back up on the tree, creating pockets for life to begin to grow again.[11]

We're all connected on an atomic level.

Bigger Than You

Connecting to something bigger than we are makes us less susceptible to the opinions and negative thoughts that follow the separate self. We become more like the ocean than a small puddle of water that's easily displaced.

It's a little counterintuitive, because our natural reaction is to place our attention on ourselves when we are struggling. We look to fix what ails us. Paradoxically, though, when we look outward rather than focusing on our self, we connect with the deeper parts of who we are. The more we focus on contributing to the whole, the more connected we feel. The more we let go of our self, the more we access our true self. This can take the form of adopting goals that are focused on something bigger than ourselves—something that contributes to the well-being or support of others or the planet.

When we apply our unique strengths and virtues toward something greater than ourselves, we recognize we are part of a larger, interrelated ecosystem. No, not in that way where you just joined a fraternity or sorority and you feel connected to a larger group. Having a purpose larger than ourselves is a portal into an awareness of the profound connectedness of all things and that we don't exist in isolation. Our attention gets drawn away from the narrow prism of our "self" to the recognition that our real nature can only be understood in context of our connection with others.

From Idea to Action

To free yourself from the narrow prism of self, develop virtues that are in service of other people. Virtues are positive ethical qualities or behaviors that have high moral standards. Virtue development forces us to recognize that we are part of an interconnected ecosystem that shifts the focus away from self and onto doing good for others. We don't cultivate virtues in isolation, but within the communities to which we belong, including family, school, teams, and work.

We develop virtues in the same way we become a good pianist or tennis player: through training and practice. Aristotle believed we become what we repeatedly do. The practice could be internal or external. Ideally, it's both. Identify a virtue you want to get better at and put a plan in place. You can choose one from the list below or come up with your own. If it's kindness, then ask, How am I going to practice kindness to others and practice kindness to self today? At the end of the day, give yourself a score and/or jot down a few notes about what you learned in your attempts to practice the expression of the desired virtue. It's that simple. Exercise the virtue muscle.

Morning prompt:

- Write down the virtue you're interested in practicing (it can be the same virtue, over and over again).

Evening prompt:

- Write down the moments in your day that you were actively engaged with the virtue.

- Reflect on specific moments (if any) that were particularly challenging for you (in relation to the virtue), how you reflexively responded, and how you'd like to respond in the future to similar events.

- List any identifiable "trip wires" (in psychology known as antecedents) to your automatic response (example: my direct report was late for our one-on-one meeting).

- Make a note of how you'd like to respond if that antecedent were to happen again that would be more aligned with the virtue that you're practicing.

- Choose from the following psychological skills that you'd like to fold into your daily practice. Choose the one or two skills that you think will help you be more consistent in expressing the virtue you're training: breathing training, confidence training, mindfulness, self-talk training, optimism training, enhancing overall recovery strategies, deep focus training.

Here is a list of virtues that pull you into relationship and out of the self trap.

Virtues

Generosity	Creativity	Gratitude
Courage	Forgiveness	Patience
Justice	Kindness	Purpose
Service	Honesty	
Humility	Respect	

PART THREE

REDEFINE

11

Challenges to Our Closely Held Beliefs

*Opinions are made to be changed—or
how is truth to be got at?*

—LORD BYRON

Research has found that we tend to discount evidence that contradicts our beliefs, but why are we so protective?[1] Why is it so difficult to change our minds when people challenge our deeply held beliefs? What goes on inside our brains during that process? What neural mechanisms get activated when someone refutes a core idea that we hold? Jonas Kaplan, an assistant research professor of psychology at the University of Southern California's Brain and Creativity Institute, ventured into the highly charged landscape of political beliefs to find out.

Kaplan led a study of forty adults that identified themselves as political liberals with deep convictions.[2] Each person was asked to read eight statements that reflected their political beliefs. For example, "The US should reduce its military budget."

After each statement, the participants read five brief contrarian statements that challenged the original viewpoint and tried to sway them—while their brains were scanned in an MRI machine. The counterarguments, like "Russia has nearly twice as many active nuclear weapons as the United States," were designed to be more provocative than factual.

The participants were also asked to read a series of nonpolitical statements like "Thomas Edison invented the light bulb." Then they were shown opposing assertions meant to raise some doubt, such as "Edison's patent for the electric light bulb was invalidated by the US Patent Office, who found that it was based on the work of another inventor."

The researchers included the nonpolitical statements to see whether there was a difference in how the brain processed challenges to people's deeply held beliefs as opposed to presumably less emotionally charged beliefs like Edison's role in history.

For the Brain, Our Most Personal Beliefs and Identity Are Indistinguishable

The study found that when participants' deeply held beliefs were challenged, there was a surge in activity in areas of the brain related to identity (default mode network), threat response (amygdala), and emotions (insular cortex, or insula). The stronger the attachment to a belief, the greater the activity in the amygdala and insula. Everyone in the study claimed to believe Edison invented the light bulb, but when they were confronted by evidence to the contrary, people generally accepted the new information and there was a reduced signal, if any, in those areas of the brain.

The results revealed remarkable insights into why other people's opinions can feel like such a threat. Challenging someone's deeply held beliefs activates the areas of the brain associated with personal identity.

An attack on the participants' political views registered as an attack on their identity, their sense of self.

For the brain, our most personal beliefs and our identity are indistinguishable.

The Brain Protects Us from Opinions That Threaten Our Identity

The brain can react to opinions that threaten our core beliefs in the same way it responds to a physical threat. The brain does not register a distinction between our physical body and our sense of self. It affords them equal protections. The brain systems responsible for protecting us kick into overdrive when the beliefs embedded in our identity are threatened by someone's opinion. As Kaplan describes it, "The brain's primary responsibility is to take care of the body, to protect the body. The psychological self is the brain's extension of that. When our self feels attacked, our [brain is] going to bring to bear the same defenses that it has for protecting the body."[3] The brain provides protection not just for our physical safety but our psychological well-being, "When the brain considers something to be part of itself, whether it's a body part or a belief, then it protects it in the same way."[4]

Evidence of the value the brain places on our identity can be found in the neurobiological security detail assigned to protect it—the insula, a part of the frontal cortex. If you have ever gulped down a mouthful of spoiled milk, eaten halfway through a slice of bread before you realized it's covered in green, fuzzy mold, or opened an outhouse door you wish you had kept closed, you've activated the insula. Putrid tastes and smells trigger a gag reflex or lurching response. Neuronal signals are sent to our face and stomach muscles and we reflexively spit out that toxic food or expunge the offending smell.

The emotion of disgust is an evolved psychological system to protect our bodies from infection through disease-avoidant behavior.[5] Humans, however, are the only animals where the insula has evolved to protect something more abstract: our identity. The part of our brain that tells us to get away from that rancid meat to protect us from a pathogen is the same mechanism that warns us against information the brain thinks may hurt our sense of self.

When other people's opinions challenge our deeply held beliefs, particularly convictions that are embedded in our sense of self, the neural networks that have evolved to protect us ramp up. The amygdala hijacks our brain before we even know what's going on. Stress hormones like adrenaline and cortisol get released that put our body on high alert. The insula gets activated. Our brain often ignores the facts out of deference to our beliefs or reshapes the facts to fit our beliefs. We cling to our worldview like our survival depends on it.

What Are We Walling In or Walling Out?

We instinctually protect our deeply held beliefs, but doing so becomes problematic when we are unwilling to entertain opposing ideas and examine the beliefs we hold. Robert Frost's poem "Mending Wall" is a poignant meditation on the barriers and beliefs that separate us—and a call to hold them up in the light.

Every spring two neighbors meet at the stone wall that separates their properties in an annual ritual to make repairs. The narrator sees no real purpose in the wall. There are no live animals to contain. Only pine trees and apple orchards line the hills.

> *Before I built a wall I'd ask to know*
> *What I was walling in or walling out*

Whenever the narrator tries to engage about the "why" behind the wall, his neighbor utters a programmed mantra inherited from his father, "Good fences make good neighbors." He has no interest in exploring his belief and whether it serves any purpose. His incurious response strikes the narrator as crude and primitive.

> *Bringing a stone grasped firmly by the top*
> *In each hand, like an old-stone savage armed.*
> *He moves in darkness as it seems to me*

We may feel better when we defend our beliefs in the face of other people's opinions, but there's value in periodically holding our beliefs up in the light. They served a purpose at some point in our life or we would not have adopted them, but are they serving us now? Take a few moments to consider at what point in your life you adopted a belief and why. Then ask whether that belief is serving you. Is it helping you reach your goals and vision for the life you want to lead? Or is the belief limiting what's possible for you?

When people challenge our deeply held beliefs, we can train the mind to recognize that it's not a threat but an opportunity.

From Idea to Action

Here's an introspective practice that is far more challenging than it sounds. If done right, it just might create space for you to become less reactive, less defensive, and more curious in situations where rigid thinking might otherwise prevail.

Take a few moments and write down a handful of beliefs that you hold to be true. Then write down a few beliefs that that you're less sure about. Now, look at the point in your life when you adopted each belief and why. How did the belief serve you at that time in your life? Now explore whether that belief is currently serving you. Is it helping you be the person you want to be? Is it helping you reach your goals and vision for the life you want to lead? Or is the belief limiting what's possible for you?

12

Look Who's Talking

The lion does not turn around when a small dog barks.

—**AFRICAN PROVERB**

At six feet two and 290 pounds, Nate Hobgood-Chittick was a massive man with an even bigger spirit for life, yet he was undersized for a defensive tackle. Nate played in the NFL for four years and won a Super Bowl with the St. Louis Rams. Nate was a dear friend. He passed away far too early at forty-six years old. We used to love talking about the spiritual life, ways to become one's very best, and how to best support and challenge others on their life adventures. He taught me a lot and I miss him just the same. I can still hear his enormous laughter and feel the way he lived life to the fullest. He loved his family, loved people, and loved life.

In his early football days, Nate described to me how some coaches would belittle, humiliate, and even threaten him. *You are so slow. I've told you a million times you are not going to make it to the next level. Why can't you just take a half-step back. It's a half-step, not a full step. What's wrong with you?* Emotionally abusive coaching can be difficult to recognize. Some athletes are willing to endure anything that might help them achieve success. They can misinterpret abusive practice as a sign their coach is interested in helping them get better. Nate saw through that. "Mike," he said to me, "you don't know what it's like to be consistently screamed at by adults in front of your friends. It was an accepted part of the culture, but it was demoralizing. I wasn't going to thrive in that kind of environment."

Nate came up with a clever tool at a young age to deal with the challenge of distinguishing opinions that raised him up from opinions that tore him down. He recognized that in order to get better he had to separate the vitriol from the valuable insights. He could not just block the coaches out, so he put up "the screen." When a coach would walk over to him or shout across the field, the only things that would come through the screen were things that would help him get better. The contempt and the negativity would stay on the coach's side.

Rather than getting caught in the trap of reflexively accepting or rejecting an opinion, Nate's screen put him in control of the process. It allowed him to hit the pause button and evaluate the merit in someone else's perspective before he responded.

Yep. The first step in reacting to the opinions of others is, well, not reacting. Take a breath. Literally.

What comes after the opinion hits the screen? How do we discern opinions that can help us learn and grow from opinions that we are still working out in therapy five years later?

We often frame the answer as a binary choice. We act like everyone's opinion matters. Or swinging to the other side of the spectrum, we say we don't care at all about anyone's opinion. They seem like diametrically opposite approaches, but they actually arrive at the same destination. If everyone's opinions matter, we lose our capacity to be open and vulnerable, to take risks and push the edges because of the concern for how we will appear. On the other hand, when we cease to care what others think, we go against the neurobiological social wiring. Either way, we end up disconnected from ourselves and the people around us.

I talked to researcher and author Brené Brown on the *Finding Mastery* podcast about an alternative path that's in line with our individual integrity and true to our inherently social nature. Brown believes that "our job becomes to get specific on whose opinions matter and find the people who love you, not despite your vulnerability, not despite your imperfection, but because of it."

Brown's primary filter for the opinions that matter is that a person must be in the arena. Somebody who is getting after it in life, who tries and fails and "whose face is marred with dust, sweat, and blood." In contrast, the opinions of those who do not step foot in the arena because they cannot control the outcome, but instead hurl "insults and criticism" from the cheap seats, will never matter.

The Roundtable

Nate's screen is a reminder that we are ultimately in control not of the opinions but whose opinions we let in and what we do with them. That begs the question, though: Whose opinions do we trust and how do we discern information that is honest, accurate, and, above all, helpful?

Rather than reacting to opinions on an ad hoc basis, you can put a strategy in place. Start by creating a roundtable of people whose opinions matter to you. Identify those two, four, eight, or ten people whose counsel you trust. They could be family members, friends, mentors, or experts. Keep the list small. The people you choose to be at your roundtable might not be Arthurian knights, but that chivalric spirit can still animate your relationships with them.

To have a seat at the roundtable, ensure that each person is committed to supporting and protecting you. In setting up your roundtable, ask yourself, Who has your back? Who really gets you, not just the refined and packaged you, but the straining, striving, and vulnerable version of you that's trying to figure out life as you go? Who has fidelity to the truth? Who can you count on to be honest with you? Who has lived a life that you respect?

Your roundtable could become the most important feedback loop in your life, but that doesn't mean that theirs are the only opinions that impact you. Whether we like it or not, every day we are inundated by opinions from friends, family members, colleagues, partners, coaches, teammates, public figures, brands, bots and strangers. If we responded to each of them, we'd have little bandwidth left for our own thoughts. Life would be a game of whack-a-mole where we were constantly attending to the opinions of others. But if we simply tried to block out all other people's opinions, we'd miss out on valuable information and opportunities to learn about ourselves. And it's not really possible to keep everyone else's opinion at bay. Some opinions find their way through the screen and stick with us and, when they do, there's generally something we can learn about ourselves.

From Idea to Action

When you have a strong immediate emotional reaction to someone's opinion, whether positive or negative, pay attention to it. Resist the temptation to override or suppress it. Your reaction is full of information about what's going on internally. Did it wash over you like a drug, confirming an idea you already held about yourself? Or did it engage your survival response and hijack your attention so your body can prepare to fight, flee, or freeze? However you respond to that opinion that penetrates your screen, the gift is in your reaction.

The next step when you get confronted by an opinion that you can't shake, or one that you hear multiple times, is to tap into the wisdom of the roundtable. Bring it to someone in your circle and see if they hold the same point of view as you. Explore it with them.

Once you receive their feedback, reflect on it. The FOPO process is constructed on the illusion that we cannot trust ourselves. Journal about it: go to that place where your thoughts are liberated from convention. Maybe it's your bedroom. Or underneath the oak tree. Or in that leather wingback chair in your favorite corner of the local Starbucks. Explore your reaction and the thinking that surrounds it. Understand what you are defending or embracing.

If you'd like a free twenty-minute mindfulness session to deepen the reflection process, please go to www.finding mastery.com/thefirstrule.

13

The Litmus Test

*Let each thing you would do, say or intend
be like that of a dying person.*

—MARCUS AURELIUS

Greatest Regret of the Dying

For eight years, Australian Bronnie Ware was an in-home caregiver who looked after people who were dying. Her clients knew they were severely ill and most were in the last three to twelve weeks of their lives. She helped them do the things they struggled to do on their own: shower, prepare meals, wipe their bottoms, organize their medications. She gradually realized, though, that the most important role she was playing was not physical but emotional. She was there to listen.

She was there to listen to her patients give what renowned German American psychologist Erik Erikson describes as "a retrospective accounting of one's life to date."[1] Erikson posited that in this eighth, and final, stage of human development, people tend to reflect back on what they have done in their lives and whether or not they are satisfied with the way they have lived and the person they have become. They come away with either a sense of fulfillment or a sense of regret and despair.

Bronnie Ware cataloged their intimate retrospections. Many more of her patients carried regrets into their last days than those who were regret free. Almost all the regrets came from a lack of courage to pursue the life they desired. Their number one regret: people wish they had the courage to live a life true to themselves rather than a life that others expected of them.

I'm going to repeat that. The greatest regret of people at the end of their lives was living for the approval of others.

When the party is almost over and everyone, and their opinions, has gone home, you'll question why you gave them so much power in your life.

We Don't Pursue What We Value Most Highly

Nobel Prize–winning economist Daniel Kahneman and a group of scientists published a study in *Science* magazine in 2004 that underscores the idea.[2] They asked nine hundred women to fill out a long diary and questionnaire detailing their daily activities and rating a range of feelings during each experience (happy, impatient, depressed, worried, tired, etc.) on a seven-point scale. The researchers compared how much satisfaction the women derived from each of the daily activities in terms of their feeling of happiness and enjoyment.

One would assume that the activities the women voluntarily had chosen would give them the greatest satisfaction. If they are choosing to do something, they must actually enjoy it, right?

Well, not exactly. The women reported getting greater satisfaction from spiritual pursuits—meditating, praying, going to church—than watching television. But they spent five times longer in front of the screen than engaging in activities that were more satisfying.

Living without a Shot Clock

There's a dissonance between the choices we want to make and the choices we actually make. Why? We don't recognize that time is the most precious of all commodities.

We live like we are going to live forever. As we part ways with people, we say, "See you later," as if it's inevitable. But we all know that one day that confident, presumptuous salutation won't be true. We have pushed our mortality to the background in Western culture. When death does occur, it's something that happens to other people. We all know we are going to die, but we don't think it's going to happen today, next week, or next year. We have crafted a view of life where death is not a reality, at least not in the foreseeable future.

The cost to living without a shot clock: it's easy to fall out of alignment with your values.

Scarcity is a widely accepted principle in behavioral sciences. When there's a limited quantity of a resource, we tend to value it more. Death creates scarcity of physical life (the time we are on this planet). How we choose to use our time becomes the most meaningful and critical decision we make over our lifetime.

Living with an awareness of our own mortality fundamentally changes what we value and how we choose to use our time.

It unmasks the frivolous, empty pursuits our culture validates. Does the response to your social media post really matter? Did it matter whether you made the post at all? Does it matter what car you drive? Does it matter if you are having a good hair day or a bad hair day? Does it matter that you are a little cleverer than most people? More intelligent? Less intelligent? Better bone structure? Does it matter that a friend group boxes you out of their social circle? If they let you in, do you really want to spend your precious time with them?

Fully embracing the fact that we are not going to live forever brings our values into sharp focus. We see with clarity what matters. When the plane suddenly drops from wind shear and we are momentarily terrified, we don't think about the wedding speech we stumbled through or the embarrassment of being fired from that job we didn't even like. When the dermatologist says she wants to biopsy the irregular-shaped mark because it looks precancerous, we are not thinking about that high-achievement image we have carefully constructed for our colleagues.

The prospect of life being interrupted, maybe permanently, dramatically shifts our perspective both on the value of time and what we value. Our minds go toward what we deeply care about. In those moments, the awareness of mortality acts as a cleansing agent, washing away everything except what matters most.

To go back to *Fight Club*, Tyler Durden (played by Brad Pitt) holds up a convenience store worker, Raymond K. Hessel, and tells him he's going to die. Durden starts flipping through the contents of Hessel's wallet, opening up a window for the audience into Hessel's unfulfilled and downbeat life story. Hessel has settled for a mediocre existence and has no motivation to

Seeing his expired student ID card, Durden cocks
~~ pistol and asks, "What did you want to be?" Hessel strug-
gles but stammers out an answer, "A vet." He wanted to be a
veterinarian but he gave it up because it was too difficult.
Durden tells Hessel he's keeping his license and promises that
if he's not on his way to being a veterinarian when he returns
in six weeks, he'll kill him.

No one needs a *Fight Club*–style enlightenment, but the
message is clear. Durden is forcing Hessel to confront his mortality in an effort to wake him, to remind all of us we don't
have time to waste.

In 2005, Apple founder/CEO Steve Jobs echoed a similar
sentiment in his candid commencement address to graduating
students at Stanford University. Jobs had been diagnosed with
a rare form of pancreatic cancer in 2003, but he was cancer-free
at the time of the speech.

> Remembering that I'll be dead soon is the most important
> tool I've ever encountered to help me make the big choices
> in life. Because almost everything—all external expecta-
> tions, all pride, all fear of embarrassment or failure—these
> things just fall away in the face of death, leaving only
> what is truly important. Remembering that you are going
> to die is the best way I know to avoid the trap of thinking
> you have something to lose. You are already naked. There
> is no reason not to follow your heart. . . .
>
> Your time is limited, so don't waste it living someone
> else's life. Don't be trapped by dogma—which is living
> with the results of other people's thinking. Don't let the
> noise of others' opinions drown out your own inner

voice. And most important, have the courage to follow your heart and intuition. They somehow already know what you truly want to become. Everything else is secondary.[3]

Jobs's awareness of his own mortality freed him up to pursue life on his own terms.

The Roman emperor and Stoic philosopher Marcus Aurelius expressed the idea even more succinctly: "You could leave life right now. Let that determine what you do and say and think."

No philosophical tradition places greater importance on reflecting on our mortality than Stoicism. The Stoics taught, almost counterintuitively, that regularly contemplating our death can dramatically improve the quality of our day-to-day lives.

In 1991, my undergraduate professor in philosophy, John Perkins, introduced me to Stoicism, and I immediately was hooked on the incredibly applied and practical nature of the Stoics' first principles. Rather than a morbid idea, the inevitability of death served a forcing function for the Stoics to be grateful for the time we have, appreciate each day, and be judicious in how we use our precious time. They were very clear in their approach to not spend time on things we cannot change (death, others' opinions, and so forth) but rather, to focus on what's 100 percent within our control (one's thoughts, words, and actions). The first rule of mastery, to work from the inside out, is marked by working toward mastering what's within our control that aligns with one's core virtues and one's purpose in life. When we die is far less important than how we want to live.

As Seneca writes in *On the Shortness of Life*:

It is not that we have a short space of time, but that we waste much of it. Life is long enough, and it has been given in sufficiently generous measure to allow the accomplishment of the very greatest things if the whole of it is well invested. But when it is squandered in luxury and carelessness, when it is devoted to no good end, forced at last by the ultimate necessity we perceive that it has passed away before we were aware that it was passing.[4]

Jeff Bezos applied a similar perspective to Amazon. At a meeting in Seattle in 2015, Bezos was asked about the future of the company in the wake of the bankruptcy of a lot of big retailers. Bezos responded, "Amazon is not too big to fail. In fact, I predict one day Amazon will fail. Amazon will go bankrupt. If you look at large companies, their lifespans tend to be 30-plus years, not a hundred-plus years."[5]

Bezos was not trying to panic shareholders and employees by reminding them Amazon has a limited lifespan. Instead, he was encouraging employees to use that awareness to let go of their anxieties about their competitors and focus on what they can control—serving the customers.

Death and Dental Pain

We might think that reminders of mortality will send us into an existential tailspin, but that's not the case. Psychologists Nathan DeWall and Roy Baumeister ran three experiments to see how people responded when contemplating their own death. About half of the 432 undergraduate volunteers were prompted to think about what it's like to be dead and write essays about what they imagined happening to them as they were dying. The other half of the students were instructed to think and write about dental pain.

When the volunteers were absorbed in thoughts of death and dying, the researchers gave them a series of word tests designed to tap into unconscious emotions. They were asked to complete word fragments such as *jo_* or *ang_ _* with letters of their choice. Some word stems were intended to elicit neutral or emotionally positive responses, such as *jog* or *joy*, while others could be filled in neutrally or negatively—*angle* versus *angry*. The results reflected the unconscious mind at work.

The researchers found that those who were thinking about their own death didn't sink into despair but became happier. Their subconscious minds generated significantly more positive word associations and feelings than the dental pain group. The researchers believe it's a psychological immune response that shields us from the threat of death.

What Will You Regret at the End of Your Life?

We don't know how long we are going to live in the physical form, so let's plan as if the great mystery is right around the corner.

Do you want to know what you will regret at the end of your life? Simply ask yourself what you regret right now. If you wish you were more present for your two-year-old daughter now, you are likely going to have that same regret four decades from now. If you regret opting for the comfort and familiarity of your current job rather than reaching for the stars, you will likely have a similar regret down the road. The big difference between now and then is that you have the ability to do something about it now.

You have a choice at every moment of your life whether you are going to play the FOPO game. Are you going to spend your precious days, hours, and moments worrying about other people's opinions? Are you going to spend your brief time on this planet worrying about what other people think you should say or do or feel?

From Idea to Action

This exercise is incredibly simple to practice. When you say goodbye to someone, say it as if you might not ever see them again. Say goodbye in a way that you demonstrate the gratitude you have for the time you have spent together.

Start with one person today. Tomorrow, two. Work your way until it becomes part of your everyday routine.

By acknowledging and embracing life's inherent fragility, we foster a genuine appreciation for the people who grace us with their presence during our brief time on this incredible planet.

Notes

Introduction

1. Cal Callahan, "Lauren Bay-Regula: Life as an Olympian, Mom, and Entrepreneur," January 28, 2020, *The Great Unlearn* podcast, https://podcasts .apple.com/us/podcast/the-great-unlearn/id1492460338?i=1000463898379.

2. When we say the greatest constrictor of human potential, we are acknowledging that the fear of getting killed, starvation, or losing your job are greater constrictors. This book is about the quality of life we live, not survival.

3. Scott Barry Kaufman, "Sailboat Metaphor," https://scottbarrykaufman.com /sailboat-metaphor.

4. Michael Gervais, "How to Stop Worrying about What Other People Think of You," hbr.org, May 2, 2019, https://hbr.org/2019/05/how-to-stop-worrying-about -what-other-people-think-of-you.

5. Lauren Regula, Instagram post, September 7, 2022.

Chapter 1

1. Quoted and translated in Alexander Wheelock Thayer, *The Life of Ludwig van Beethoven: Vol. 1* [1866], ed. Henry Edward Krehbiel (New York: The Beethoven Association, 1921), 300.

2. Thayer, *Life of Beethoven*, 300.

3. Heiligenstadt Testament, a letter written by Beethoven to his brothers Carl and Johann on October 6, 1802, http://www.lvbeethoven.com/Bio/Biography HeiligenstadtTestament.html.

4. Jan Swafford, *Beethoven: Anguish and Triumph; A Biography* (Boston: Houghton Mifflin Harcourt, 2014), 428; H. C. Robbins Landon, *Beethoven: A Documentary Story* (New York: Macmillan, 1974), 210. Lichnowsky's physician, Dr. Anton Weiser, tells the story of when Beethoven was offended by being asked to play the violin at a dinner.

5. Swafford, *Beethoven*, 21.

6. Swafford, *Beethoven*, 53.

7. Franz Wegeler and Ferdinand Ries, *Beethoven Remembered: The Biographical Notes of Franz Wegeler and Ferdinand Ries* (Salt Lake City, UT: Great River Books, 1987), 39.

8. Swafford, *Beethoven*, 98–99.

9. Swafford, *Beethoven*, 128. "Part of his gift was the *raptus*, that ability to withdraw into an inner world that took him beyond everything and everybody around him, and also took him beyond the legion of afflictions that assailed him. Improvising at the keyboard and otherwise, he found solitude even in company."

10. Swafford, *Beethoven*, 98–99.

11. Heiligenstadt Testament letter.

12. David Ryback, *Beethoven in Love* (Andover, MA: Tiger Iron Press, 1996). Quote is from Beethoven in 1817.

13. Nicholas Cook, *Beethoven: Symphony No. 9* (Cambridge, UK: Cambridge University Press, 1993).

Chapter 2

1. Michael Gervais, "Tune Up Your Mind—A Music Legend's Journey of Self-Evolution," *Finding Mastery* podcast, June 28, 2023, https://findingmastery.com/podcasts/moby-lindsay/.

2. This echoes a quote often attributed to Austrian psychiatrist and Holocaust survivor Viktor Frankl, but is of uncertain origins: "Between stimulus and response there is a space. In that space is our power to choose our response. In our response lies our growth and our freedom."

3. Mark Leary, "Is It Time to Give Up on Self-Esteem?," The Society for Personality and Social Psychology, May 9, 2019, https://spsp.org/news-center/character-context-blog/it-time-give-self-esteem.

Chapter 3

1. N. C. Larson et al., "Physiological Reactivity and Performance Outcomes under High Pressure in Golfers of Varied Skill Levels," oral presentation to the World Scientific Congress of Golf, Phoenix, AZ, March 2012.

2. Thomas Hobbes, *Leviathan*, part 1, chapter 13, page 58.

3. W. B. Cannon, *Bodily Changes in Pain, Hunger, Fear, and Rage: An Account of Recent Researches into the Function of Emotional Excitement* (New York: D. Appleton and Company, 1915); Keith Oatley, Dacher Keltner, and Jennifer M. Jenkins, *Understanding Emotions*, 2nd ed. (Hoboken, NJ: Wiley-Blackwell Publishing, 2006).

4. Cannon, *Bodily Changes in Pain, Hunger, Fear, and Rage*.

5. Cannon, *Bodily Changes in Pain, Hunger, Fear, and Rage*.

6. Cannon, *Bodily Changes in Pain, Hunger, Fear, and Rage*.

7. Cannon, *Bodily Changes in Pain, Hunger, Fear, and Rage*.

8. Stephanie A. Maddox, Jakob Hartmann, Rachel A. Ross, and Kerry J. Ressler, "Deconstructing the Gestalt: Mechanisms of Fear, Threat, and Trauma Memory Encoding," *Neuron* 102, no. 1 (2019): 60–74.

9. Joseph E. LeDoux, "Coming to Terms with Fear," *PNAS* 111, no. 8 (2014): 2871–2878.

10. Josephine Germer, Evelyn Kahl, and Markus Fendt, "Memory Generalization after One-Trial Contextual Fear Conditioning: Effects of Sex and Neuropeptide S Receptor Deficiency," *Behavioural Brain Research* 361, no. 1 (2019): 159–166; Kim Haesen, Tom Beckers, Frank Baeyens, and Bram Vervliet, "One-Trial Overshadowing: Evidence for Fast Specific Fear Learning in Humans," *Behaviour Research and Therapy* 90 (2017): 16–24.

11. Roy F. Baumeister, Ellen Bratslavsky, Catrin Finkenauer, and Kathleen D. Vohs, "Bad Is Stronger Than Good," *Review of General Psychology* 5, no. 4 (2001): 323–370.

12. Arun Asok, Eric R. Kandel, and Joseph B. Rayman, "The Neurobiology of Fear Generalization," *Frontiers in Behavioral Neuroscience* 12 (2019).

13. David Watson and Ronald Friend, "Measurement of Social-Evaluative Anxiety," *Journal of Consulting and Clinical Psychology* 33, no. 4 (1969): 448–457.

Chapter 4

1. Brad Rock, quoted in David Fleming, "Before 'The Last Dance,' Scottie Pippen Delivered Six Words of Trash Talk That Changed NBA History," ESPN, May 15, 2020, https://www.espn.com/nba/story/_/id/29166548/before-last-dance -scottie-pippen-delivered-six-words-trash-talk-changed-nba-history.

2. Nina Strohminger, Joshua Knobe, and George Newman, "The True Self: A Psychological Concept Distinct from the Self," *Association for Psychological Science* 12, no. 4 (2017): 551–560.

3. Michael A. Hogg and Dominic Abrams, *Social Identifications: A Social Psychology of Intergroup Relations and Group Processes* (London: Routledge, 1998).

4. *Fight Club*, directed by David Fincher, 1999.

5. Lewis Carroll, *Alice's Adventures in Wonderland* (New York, Boston: T. Y. Crowell & Co., 1893).

6. APA Dictionary of Psychology.

7. Paul Blake, "What's in a Name? Your Link to the Past," BBC, April 26, 2011, https://www.bbc.co.uk/history/familyhistory/get_started/surnames_01 .shtml.

8. Zygmunt Bauman, "Identity in the Globalising World," *Social Anthropology* 9, no. 2 (2001): 121–129; Anthony Giddens, *The Consequences of Modernity* (Stanford, CA: Stanford University Press, 1991).

9. Jeffrey J. Arnett, "The Psychology of Globalization," *American Psychologist* 57, no. 10 (2002): 774–783.

10. Michael Lipka, "Why America's 'Nones' Left Religion Behind," Pew Research Center, August 24, 2016, https://www.pewresearch.org/fact-tank/2016/08 /24/why-americas-nones-left-religion-behind/.

11. The ten-thousand-hour rule popularized by Malcom Gladwell does not accurately align with Anders Ericsson's original research on developing expertise.

12. Nadia Shafique, Seema Gul, and Seemab Raseed, "Perfectionism and Perceived Stress: The Role of Fear of Negative Evaluation," *International Journal of Mental Health* 46, no. 4 (2017): 312–326.

13. Conversation with Dr. Ben Houltberg, March 9, 2021.

14. Albert Bandura, *Self-Efficacy: The Exercise of Control* (New York: W. H. Freeman and Company, 1997), 3.

15. Michael Gervais, "Missy Franklin on Being a Champion in Victory and Defeat," *Finding Mastery* podcast, December 4, 2019, https://podcasts.apple.com /kw/podcast/missy-franklin-on-being-a-champion-in-victory-and-defeat /id1025326955?i=1000458624052.

16. Benjamin W. Walker and Dan V. Caprar, "When Performance Gets Personal: Towards a Theory of Performance-Based Identity," *The Tavistock Institute* 73, no. 8 (2019): 1077–1105.

17. Joseph Campbell, *Reflections on the Art of Living: A Joseph Campbell Companion* (New York: Harper Perennial, 1995).

18. Dan Gilbert, "The Psychology of Your Future Self," TED talk, 2014, https://www.ted.com/talks/dan_gilbert_the_psychology_of_your_future_self.

19. Jordi Quoidbach, Daniel T. Gilbert, and Timothy D. Wilson, "The End of History Illusion," *Science* 339, no. 6115 (2013): 96–98.

20. Robbie Hummel and Jeff Goodman, "Jim Nantz Joins 68 Shining Moments to Discuss His Most Famous Calls, Giving Out Ties and His Favorite March Memories," *68 Shining Moments* podcast, March 2021, https://open.spotify.com /episode/3EbQCv7eHwSdVOQCPqQUeL.

Chapter 5

1. William James, "The Conscious Self," in William James, *The Principles of Psychology*, vol. 1 (Boston: Harvard University Press, 1892).

2. Jennifer Crocker and Connie T. Wolfe, "Contingencies of Self-Worth," *Psychological Review* 108, no. 3 (2001): 593–623.

3. Crocker and Wolfe, "Contingencies of Self-Worth."

4. Jennifer Crocker, "The Costs of Seeking Self-Esteem," *Journal of Social Issues* 58, no. 3 (2002): 597–615.

5. Crocker, "The Costs of Seeking Self-Esteem."

6. Charles S. Carver and Michael F. Scheier, *On the Self-Regulation of Behavior* (Cambridge, UK: Cambridge University Press, 1998); Jennifer Crocker and Lora E. Park, "Seeking Self-Esteem: Construction, Maintenance, and Protection of Self-Worth," University of Michigan working paper, January 1, 2003.

7. Roy F. Baumeister, Ellen Bratslavsky, Mark Muraven, and Dianne M. Tice, "Ego Depletion: Is the Active Self a Limited Resource?," *Journal of Personality and Social Psychology* 74, no. 5 (1998): 1252–1265; Roy F. Baumeister, Brad J. Bushman, and W. Keith Campbell, "Self-Esteem, Narcissism, and Aggression: Does Violence Result from Low Self-Esteem or from Threatened Egotism?," *Current*

Directions in Psychological Science 9, no. 1 (2000): 26–29; Michael H. Kernis and Stefanie B. Waschull, "The Interactive Roles of Stability and Level of Self-Esteem: Research and Theory," in Mark P. Zanna (ed.), *Advances in Experimental Social Psychology*, vol. 27 (Cambridge, MA: Academic Press, 1995), 93–141.

8. Rick Hanson, *Buddha's Brain: The Practical Neuroscience of Love, Happiness and Wisdom* (Oakland, CA: New Harbinger Publications, 2009).

9. Albert Bandura, *Social Learning Theory* (Englewood Cliffs, NJ: Prentice Hall, 1977).

10. Avi Assor, Guy Roth, and Edward L. Deci, "The Emotional Costs of Parents' Conditional Regard: A Self-Determination Theory Analysis," *Journal of Personality* 72, no. 1 (2004): 47–88.

11. Ece Mendi and Jale Eldeleklioğlu, "Parental Conditional Regard, Subjective Well-Being and Self-Esteem: The Mediating Role of Perfectionism," *Psychology* 7, no. 10 (2016): 1276–1295.

12. Dare A. Baldwin and Louis J. Moses, "Early Understanding of Referential Intent and Attentional Focus: Evidence from Language and Emotion," in Charlie Lewis and Peter Mitchell (eds.), *Children's Early Understanding of Mind: Origins and Development* (Hillsdale, NJ: Lawrence Erlbaum Associates, 1994), 133–156; Richard M. Ryan, Edward L. Deci, and Wendy S. Grolnick, "Autonomy, Relatedness, and the Self: Their Relation to Development and Psychopathology," in Dante Cicchetti and Donald J. Cohen (eds.), *Developmental Psychopathology, Volume 1: Theory and Method* (Hoboken, NJ: John Wiley and Sons, 1995), 618–665; Susan Harter, "Causes and Consequences of Low Self-Esteem in Children and Adolescents," in Roy Baumeister (ed.) *Self-Esteem: The Puzzle of Low Self-Regard* (New York: Plenum Press, 1993), 87–116.

13. Tim Kasser, Richard M. Ryan, Charles E. Couchman, and Kennon M. Sheldon, "Materialistic Values: Their Causes and Consequences," in Tim Kasser and Allen D. Kanner (eds.), *Psychology and Consumer Culture: The Struggle for a Good Life in a Materialistic World* (Washington, DC: American Psychological Association, 2004), 11–28.

14. Rory Sutherland, "Life Lessons from an Ad Man," TED talk, 2008, https://www.ted.com/talks/rory_sutherland_life_lessons_from_an_ad_man.

Chapter 6

1. Timothy D. Wilson et al., "Just Think: The Challenges of the Disengaged Mind," *Science* 345, no. 6192 (2014): 75–77.

2. Not to be confused with Depeche Mode, an electronic music band from the 1980s.

3. Marcus Raichle interviewed by Svend Davanger, "The Brain's Default Mode Network—What Does It Mean to Us?," *The Meditation Blog*, March 9, 2015, https://www.themeditationblog.com/the-brains-default-mode-network-what-does-it-mean-to-us/.

4. Randy L. Buckner, "The Serendipitous Discovery of the Brain's Default Network," *Neuroimage* 62 (2012): 1137–1147.

5. Marcus E. Raichle and Abraham Z. Snyder, "A Default Mode of Brain Function: A Brief History of an Evolving Idea," *Neuroimage* 37 (2007): 1083–1090.

6. Raichle interview, "Brain's Default Mode."

7. Marcus E. Raichle and Debra A. Gusnard, "Appraising the Brain's Energy Budget," *PNAS* 99, no. 16 (2002): 10237–10239; Camila Pulido and Timothy A. Ryan, "Synaptic Vesicle Pools Are a Major Hidden Resting Metabolic Burden of Nerve Terminals," *Science Advances* 7, no. 49 (2021).

8. Matthew A. Killingsworth and Daniel T. Gilbert, "A Wandering Mind Is an Unhappy Mind," *Science* 330, no. 6006 (2010): 932.

9. Barbara Tomasino, Sara Fregona, Miran Skrap, and Franco Fabbro, "Meditation-Related Activations Are Modulated by the Practices Needed to Obtain It and by the Expertise: An ALE Meta-Analysis Study," *Human Neuroscience* 6 (2012); Judson A. Brewer et al., "Meditation Experience Is Associated with Differences in Default Mode Network Activity and Connectivity," *PNAS* 108, no. 50 (2011): 20254–20259.

10. Jon Kabat-Zinn, "Some Reflections on the Origins of MBSR, Skillful Means, and the Trouble with Maps," *Contemporary Buddhism* 12, no. 1 (2011): 281–306.

11. Jon Kabat-Zinn, "Mindfulness-Based Interventions in Context: Past, Present, and Future," *Clinical Psychology: Science and Practice* 10, no. 2 (2003): 144–156.

Chapter 7

1. Thomas Gilovich, Victoria H. Medvec, and Kenneth Savitsky, "The Spotlight Effect in Social Judgment: An Egocentric Bias in Estimates of the Salience of One's Own Actions and Appearance," *Journal of Personality and Social Psychology* 78, no. 2 (2000): 211–222.

2. Gilovich, Medvec, and Savitsky, "Spotlight Effect in Social Judgment."

3. Gilovich, Medvec, and Savitsky, "Spotlight Effect in Social Judgment."

4. Thomas Gilovich, "Differential Construal and the False Consensus Effect," *Journal of Personality and Social Psychology* 59, no. 4 (1990): 623–634.

5. Amos Tversky and Daniel Kahneman, "Judgment under Uncertainty: Heuristics and Biases," *Science* 185, no. 4157 (1974): 1124–1131.

Chapter 8

1. "Theory of Mind," Harvard Medical School News and Research, January 27, 2021, https://hms.harvard.edu/news/theory-mind.

2. William Ickes, "Everyday Mind Reading Is Driven by Motives and Goals," *Psychological Inquiry* 22, no. 3 (2011): 200–206.

3. Nicholas Epley, *Mindwise: Why We Misunderstand What Others Think, Believe, Feel, and Want* (New York: Vintage, 2015).

4. Epley, *Mindwise*.

5. Belinda Luscombe, "10 Questions for Daniel Kahneman," *Time*, November 28, 2011, https://content.time.com/time/magazine/article /0,9171,2099712,00.html.

6. Tal Eyal, Mary Steffel, and Nicholas Epley, "Perspective Mistaking: Accurately Understanding the Mind of Another Requires Getting Perspective, Not Taking Perspective," *Journal of Personality and Social Psychology* 114, no. 4 (2018): 547–571.

7. Dale Carnegie, *How to Win Friends and Influence People* (New York: Simon & Schuster, 2009).

8. Nicholas Epley, "We All Think We Know the People We Love. We're All Deluded," *Invisibilia*, NPR, March 22, 2018, https://www.npr.org/sections/health -shots/2018/03/22/594023688/invisibilia-to-understand-another-s-mind-get -perspective-don-t-take-it.

9. V. S. Ramachandran, *A Brief Tour of Human Consciousness* (New York: Pi Press, 2004), 3.

10. Epley, "We All Think We Know the People We Love."

11. Erving Goffman, *The Presentation of Self in Everyday Life* (New York: Anchor Books, 1959).

Chapter 9

1. Leo Benedictus, "#Thedress: 'It's Been Quite Stressful to Deal with It . . . We Had a Falling-Out,'" *Guardian*, December 22, 2015, https://www.theguardian .com/fashion/2015/dec/22/thedress-internet-divided-cecilia-bleasdale-black-blue -white-gold.

2. "Optical Illusion: Dress Colour Debate Goes Global," BBC News, February 27, 2015, https://www.bbc.com/news/uk-scotland-highlands-islands -31656935; Benedictus, "#Thedress"; Terrence McCoy, "The Inside Story of the 'White Dress, Blue Dress' Drama That Divided a Planet," *Washington Post*, February 27, 2015, https://www.washingtonpost.com/news/morning-mix/wp/2015 /02/27/the-inside-story-of-the-white-dress-blue-dress-drama-that-divided-a-nation /; Claudia Koerner, "The Dress Is Blue and Black, Says the Girl Who Saw It in Person," BuzzFeed News, February 26, 2015, https://www.buzzfeednews.com /article/claudiakoerner/the-dress-is-blue-and-black-says-the-girl-who-saw-it-in-pers.

3. Pascal Wallisch, "Illumination Assumptions Account for Individual Differences in the Perceptual Interpretation of a Profoundly Ambiguous Stimulus in the Color Domain: 'The Dress,'" *Journal of Vision* 17, no. 4 (2017): 5; Christoph Witzel, Chris Racey, J. Kevin O'Regan, "The Most Reasonable Explanation of 'The Dress': Implicit Assumptions about Illumination," *Journal of Vision* 17, no. 2 (2017): 1.

4. Chris Shelton, "Let's Get into Neuroscience with Dr. Jonas Kaplan," *Sensibly Speaking* podcast, https://www.youtube.com/watch?v=_dPl6NKI1M4, 41:00.

5. Jonas Kaplan, "This Is How You Achieve Lasting Change by Rewiring Your Beliefs," Impact Theory, November 25, 2021, https://impacttheory.com/episode /jonas-kaplan/.

6. Christopher Chabris and Daniel Simons, *The Invisible Gorilla: And Other Ways Our Intuitions Deceive Us* (New York: Crown Publishers, 2011).

7. James Alcock, *Belief: What It Means to Believe and Why Our Convictions Are So Compelling* (Amherst, NY: Prometheus Books, 2018).

8. Joshua Klayman and Young-won Ha, "Confirmation, Disconfirmation, and Information in Hypothesis Testing," *Psychological Review* 94, no. 2 (1987): 211–228.

9. Richard E. Nisbett and Timothy D. Wilson, "Telling More Than We Can Know: Verbal Reports on Mental Processes," *Psychological Review* 84, no. 3 (1977): 231–259.

10. Francis Bacon, *The New Organon, or True Directions Concerning the Interpretation of Nature*, 1620.

11. Drake Baer, "Kahneman: Your Cognitive Biases Act Like Optical Illusions," *New York* magazine, January 13, 2017, https://www.thecut.com/2017/01 /kahneman-biases-act-like-optical-illusions.html.

12. Baer, "Kahneman."

Chapter 10

1. Jeff Pearlman, *Love Me, Hate Me: Barry Bonds and the Making of an Antihero* (New York: HarperCollins: 2006); Jeff Pearlman, "For Bonds, Great Wasn't Good Enough," ESPN, March 14, 2006, https://www.espn.com/mlb/news /story?id=2368395.

2. A. W. Tucker, "The Mathematics of Tucker: A Sampler," *The Two-Year College Mathematics Journal* 14, no. 3 (1983): 228–232.

3. Varda Liberman, Steven M. Samuels, and Lee Ross, "The Name of the Game: Predictive Power of Reputations versus Situational Labels in Determining Prisoner's Dilemma Game Moves," *Personality and Social Psychology Bulletin* 30, no. 9 (2004): 1175–1185.

4. Matthew Lieberman, "The Social Brain and the Workplace," Talks at Google, February 4, 2019, https://www.youtube.com/watch?v=h7UR9JwQEYk.

5. Alexis de Tocqueville, *Democracy in America, Volume II*, translated by Henry Reeve, 1840.

6. Mark Manson, "9 Steps to Hating Yourself a Little Less," Mark Manson blog, August 26, 2016, https://markmanson.net/hate-yourself.

7. Richard Schiffman, "We Need to Relearn That We're a Part of Nature, Not Separate from It," billmoyers.com, March 2, 2015.

8. Scott Galloway, "The Myth—and Liability—of America's Obsession with Rugged Individualism," Marker, March 15, 2021, https://medium.com/marker/the -myth-and-liability-of-americas-obsession-with-rugged-individualism-cf0ba80c2a05.

9. Roy F. Baumeister and Mark R. Leary, "The Need to Belong: Desire for Interpersonal Attachments as a Fundamental Human Motivation," *Psychological Bulletin* 117, no. 3 (1995): 497–529.

10. Baumeister and Leary, "The Need to Belong."

11. Jonathan White, *Talking on the Water: Conversations about Nature and Creativity* (San Antonio, TX: Trinity University Press, 2016).

Chapter 11

1. Charles G. Lord, Lee Ross, and Mark R. Lepper, "Biased Assimilation and Attitude Polarization: The Effects of Prior Theories on Subsequently Considered Evidence," *Journal of Personality and Social Psychology* 37, no. 11 (1979): 2098–2109.

2. Jonas T. Kaplan, Sarah I. Gimbel, and Sam Harris, "Neural Correlates of Maintaining One's Political Beliefs in the Face of Counterevidence," *Scientific Reports* 6 (2016): 39589.

3. Brian Resnick, "A New Brain Study Sheds Light on Why It Can Be So Hard to Change Someone's Political Beliefs," Vox, January 23, 2017, https://www .vox.com/science-and-health/2016/12/28/14088992/brain-study-change-minds.

4. Jacqueline Howard, "This Is Why You Get Worked Up about Politics, According to Science," CNN, January 3, 2017, https://www.cnn.com/2017/01/03 /health/political-beliefs-brain/index.html.

5. Valerie Curtis, Mícheál de Barra, and Robert Aunger, "Disgust as an Adaptive System for Disease Avoidance Behaviour," *Philosophical Transactions of the Royal Society B* 366, no. 1563 (2011): 389–401.

Chapter 13

1. Erik Erikson, *The Life Cycle Completed* (New York: W. W. Norton, 1982), 112.

2. Daniel Kahneman et al., "A Survey Method for Characterizing Daily Life Experience: The Day Reconstruction Method," *Science* 306, no. 5702 (2004): 1776–1780; Daniel Kahneman et al., "The Day Reconstruction Method (DRM): Instrument Documentation," July 2004, https://dornsife.usc.edu/assets/sites/780 /docs/drm_documentation_july_2004.pdf.

3. Steve Jobs, Commencement Address, Stanford University, June 12, 2005, https://news.stanford.edu/2005/06/14/jobs-061505/.

4. Seneca, *On the Shortness of Life*.

5. Eugene Kim, "'One Day, Amazon Will Fail' but Our Job Is to Delay It as Long as Possible," CNBC, November 15, 2018.

Index

acceptance, 21–22, 32–33
acceptance and commitment therapy
    (ACT), 53
adrenaline, 49, 170
advertising, 97
Alcock, James, 139–140
Alice's Adventures in Wonderland
    (Carroll), 68
alignment, 181
Allen, Hillary, 87–88
Amazon, 185
amygdala, 49, 168–169, 170
anchoring and adjustment, 116–117, 141
anticipation, in FOPO, 33–37, 78
anxiety
    cost of, 54, 94
    preperformance, 123–124
approval, 82–84
    Beethoven and, 18–19
    regrets based on seeking, 179–187
assumptions, 73
    perception and, 138–139
athletes, 8–9
    emotional abuse of, 173–174
    Fowler, Rickie, 45–47
    Franklin, Missy, 76
    Malone, Karl, 63–66
    performance driver for, 71
    Regula, Lauren, 1–3, 4
    sports psychology and, 122–125
    steroid use among, 149–150
attention
    inattentional blindness and, 139
    mindfulness and, 106–110

mind-wandering and, 105–106
    of others on us, 113–120
attentional costs, 37, 39, 46–47
Aurelius, Marcus, 179, 184
authenticity, 40
autonomy, 92
awareness
    of FOPO, 12–13
    mindfulness and, 108
    of mortality, 179–187
    self-worth and, 98–99

Bacon, Francis, 142–143
Baumeister, Roy, 158–159, 185–186
Baumgartner, Felix, 9
Beethoven, Johann von, 18–19
Beethoven, Ludwig von, 15–25
    facing his fears by, 20–22
    inner world of, 19–20
    letting go of control by, 23–24
    Ninth Symphony, 24
    relationship with father, 18–19
beliefs
    challenges to, 167–172
    confirmation bias and, 142–145
    curiosity and, 145–146
    examining your, 172
    as filters for perception, 140–141
    identity and, 169–170
    perception and, 137–148
belonging, the need for, 152–153, 158–159
    myth of self-reliance and, 158
Bergoglio, Jorge Mario, 68

Bezos, Jeff, 185
biases
  confirmation, 142–145
  curiosity versus, 146
  egocentric, 114–115
  perception and, 140–141, 146–148
Biosphere 2, 82
Bleasdale, Cecilia, 137–138, 139
blindness, inattentional, 139
Bonds, Barry, 149–150
bottom-up processing, 138–139
brain
  anchoring and adjustment and, 116–117
  being alone with your thoughts and,
    101–103
  default mode network in, 103–105
  external validation and, 91–92
  fear and, 48
  heuristics used by, 144–145
  neurobiology of FOPO and, 101–110
  perception and, 138–140
  reflexes and, 48–50
  responding to challenged beliefs
    and, 167–172
  wandering thoughts and, 105–106
Brown, Brené, 175
Buffett, Warren, 137
butterflies in your stomach, 49
Byron, Lord, 167

Campbell, Joseph, 78
Carnegie, Dale, 132
Carroll, Lewis, 68
change
  in identity, 67–69
  learner's mindset and, 79–82
  pain as impetus for, 21–22
checking phase of FOPO, 37–39
Chicago Bulls, 63–66
classical conditioning, 51–52
cognitive behavioral therapy (CBT), 53
communication, 38–39

challenged beliefs and, 167–172
  emotionally abusive, 173–174
  knowing what others think and,
    125–127, 132–134
community game, 151
comparisons, 23, 79
Conan Doyle, Arthur, 121
conditional regard, 95–96
conditioning, 51–52
confirmation bias, 142–145
confrontation, 40–41
connection, 152–153, 158–164
  to something bigger than you, 161–162
contemplative mindfulness, 108
contingencies of self-worth, 90–91
control, 118
  determining what you can and can't,
    24–25
  focusing on what you can, 46–47
  systematic desensitization and, 56–58
  wasting resources on attempts at, 23–24
  what is and isn't in your control and,
    10–11
core values, 84–85
cortisol, 170
creativity, wandering thoughts and, 106
criticism, 9–10
Crocker, Jennifer, 90–91
cues
  checking for, 33, 34, 37–39, 42
  responding to perceived, 39–41
curiosity, 81–82, 145–146
  challenged beliefs and, 170–172

Damon, Matt, 82
death
  living with awareness of, 179–187
  regrets and, 179–180
Deci, Ed, 92
decision-making
  FOPO as a filter in, 34–35
  on how to respond to things, 30–31

default mode network (DMN), 103–105,
    168–169
dental pain, 185–186
Denver Broncos, 9
Deseret News, 64
DeWall, Nathan, 185–186
disgust, 170
DMN. *See* default mode network (DMN)
Donne, John, 149
dopamine, 91–92
duck-rabbit illusion, 143

egocentrism, 114–115
Ellen DeGeneres Show, 138
Emerson, Ralph Waldo, 107
emotional health, sociability and, 31–33
end of history illusion, 80–81
environment
    creation of safe, 53
    scanning for cues, 33, 34, 37–39,
        42, 94–95
    separating ourselves from, 157
Epley, Nicholas, 130, 132, 133
Erikson, Erik, 179–180
evolution
    fear and, 47–50
    the need for belonging and, 151–152,
        158–161
excellence, pursuit of, 72–73
exercises
    on bias and perception, 147–148
    on challenging beliefs, 172
    decoupling identity from approval,
        84–85
    to determine what you can and can't
        control, 24–25
    on the FOPO loop, 42–43
    mindfulness, 109–110
    in mind reading, 134–136
    on responding to opinions, 177
    on saying goodbye, 187
    on self-worth awareness, 98–99

on the spotlight effect, 119–120
    virtues and, 162–164
experiences, embedding of positive
        versus negative, 51–52
externalization of value, 5
    validation and, 29–31
Eyal, Tal, 132, 133

false consensus effect, 116
fear, 45–61
    conditioning of, 51–52
    of failure, 72–73
    function of, 47–48
    learning, 50
    measuring, 60–61
    reflexes and, 48–50
    systematic desensitization for, 53–60
    triggers, hierarchy of, 56
Fear of Negative Evaluation Sale (FNE), 60
feedback
    conditional self-worth and, 93–94
    roundtables for, 175–176
    sense of self and, 81–82
Fight Club, 67–68, 182–183
Finding Mastery podcast, 76, 87–88,
        126, 175
Florida State University, 84
focus, 46–47, 182–183
FOPO (fear of people's opinions), 3–5
    anticipation phase in, 35–37
    avoiding regrets and, 179–187
    checking phase in, 37–39
    consequences of, 5–6
    defining characteristics of, 33–35
    facing, 20–22
    fear factors in, 45–61
    identity and, 63–85
    knowing others' thoughts and, 121–136
    leaning into, 11–13
    loop of, 35–44
    mechanics of, 29–44
    need for belonging and, 152

FOPO (*continued*)
  neurobiology of, 101–110
  on-ramps to, 41–43
  outsourcing self-worth and, 87–99
  passivity, projection, and, 134
  as preemptive process, 140–141
  resources used by, 34–35
  responding phase in, 39–41
  role of our beliefs in, 140–141
  separate versus social self and, 149–164
  spotlight effect and, 113–120
  success and vulnerability to, 9–10
foreclosure, identity, 75–76
Fowler, Rickie, 45–47
Francis (pope), 68
Franklin, Missy, 76
Friend, Ronald, 60
Frost, Robert, 170–171
functional magnetic resonance imaging
  (fMRI), 103–104

Galloway, Scott, 158
game theory, 150
genius, myth of the lone, 158
geographic mobility, 154
Gilbert, Dan, 80–81, 105–106
Gilovich, Thomas, 113–114, 115
goals, 152
  mind-wandering and, 105–106
  regrets and, 180–181
  self-esteem and, 89
Goodall, Jane, 121
Griffey, Ken, Jr., 149–150

Hamilton, Leonard, 84
Hanson, Rick, 95
Heiligenstadt Testament (Beethoven),
  20–21
heuristics, 144–145
hierarchy of fear triggers, 56
Hitchcock, Alfred, 140

Hobgood-Chittick, Nate, 173–174
Hoburg, Woody, 7–8
Houltberg, Ben, 72, 73–74, 77, 83–84
*How to Win Friends and Influence
  People* (Carnegie), 132
hypervigilance, 34, 48, 94–95
hypothalamus, 49, 91–92

ideas to action, 24–25
identity, 63–85
  Beethoven's deafness and, 17–18
  challenged beliefs and, 169–170
  decoupling from approval, 84–85
  definition of, 66–67
  foreclosure, 75–76
  historical, 69–70
  instability of performance-based, 74–78
  learner's mindset and, 79–82
  organizational, 71–72
  as pattern of thoughts, 73–74
  performance-based, 42–43, 69–78
  poor sense of self and, 41–43
  professional, 71–72
  purpose and, 82–84
  self-protection and, 77–78
  sense of self and, 78–79
  sources of, 67–68
illusion, duck-rabbit, 143
imagery, 123–124
impostor syndrome, 156
inattentional blindness, 139
individualism, 158
insular cortex, 168–169, 170
International Space Station, 8
interpersonal expectancy effect, 141
isolation, 16, 18, 22, 162

James, William, 89
Jastrow, Joseph, 143–144
Jennings, Kerri Walsh, 9
Jobs, Steve, 183–184

Jordan, Michael, 63
judgment of others, 113–120
Jung, Carl, 1, 63

Kabat-Zinn, Jon, 107
Kahneman, Daniel, 116, 131–132,
   143–144, 180
Kaplan, Jonas, 167–169
Killingsworth, Matthew, 105–106

Lao Tzu, 24
leaders and leadership, 70
   scrutiny of, 10
   self-reliance and, 158
learner's mindset, 79–82
learning
   conditional self-worth, 95–97
   of fears, 48–52
   from FOPO, 11–12
   mindfulness, 107–110
Leary, Mark, 32–33, 158–159
Liberman, Varda, 151
Lichnowsky, Prince, 17
Lieberman, Matthew, 151
Lindbergh, Charles, 121
locative names, 69
loneliness, 152–153

Malone, Karl, 63–66
Mandela, Nelson, 45
Manilow, Barry, 113–114
Manson, Mark, 156
Margulis, Lynn, 160–161
The Martian (film), 82
mastery, 6
   constant pursuit of, 9–10
   control and, 10–11
   metrics for, 23
   the path of, 22–24
   technical excellence versus, 23

Matisse, Henri, 15
May-Treanor, Misty, 9
McGwire, Mark, 149–150
McNeill, Caitlin, 137–138
meaning, 157, 181
   connecting to something bigger
      than you and, 161–162
   purpose and, 83–84
   understanding others', 129, 132
media, 125–126
meetings, 77, 94, 160
   anticipatory FOPO in, 35–37
memories
   fear and, 50–52
   identity and, 67
   wandering minds and, 105
"Mending Wall" (Frost), 170–171
mental health, sociability and,
   31–33
mental states, inferring others', 129–132
metrics
   for FOPO, 60–61
   for mastery, 23
   performance-based identity and, 74
   of self-worth, 89–90
   for success, 10
   technology and, 71
mindfulness, 106–110
   contemplative, 108
   practicing, 109–110
   single-point, 108, 109–110
Mindfulness-Based Stress Reduction
   (MBSR), 107
mind reading, 121–136
   inaccuracy of, 132–134
   testing your skills at, 134–136
mindset, 46–47
   learner's, 79–82
mixed martial arts (MMA), 123–124
Moby, 29–31
mortality, living with awareness of,
   179–187
mountain rescues, 7–8

names, identity and, 69–70
Nantz, Jim, 84
NASA, 8
nature, disconnection from, 157
neurobiology of FOPO, 101–110
nicknames, 69

occupational names, 69
Olympics, 1–3, 4, 9, 76
On the Shortness of Life (Seneca), 184–185
opinions
    being curious about, 81–82
    evaluating others', 173–177
    overvaluing others', 33
    public, 10, 31
    See also FOPO (fear of people's
        opinions)
organizational identity, 72
overconfidence, 131–132

passivity, 134
patronymic names, 69
Pavlov, Ivan, 51
perception, 137–148
    biases and, 146–148
    confirmation bias and, 142–145
    construction of, 138–140
    curiosity and, 145–146
    filters in, 140–141
    of others' thoughts, 121–136
    self-worth and, 97
perfectionism, 72–73
performance-based identity, 42–43, 69–78
    defining factors of, 72–73
    identity foreclosure and, 75–76
    instability of, 74–78
Perkins, John, 184
Pippen, Scottie, 64, 65
political beliefs, 167–169
popular culture, 71–72
positron emission tomography (PET), 104

potential, 6, 7–8
pressure test, 45–47
prisoner's dilemma, 150
problem-solving, 104–105
professional identity, 71–72
projection, 134
protection of self, 5, 31
    by Beethoven, 18
    conditional self-worth and, 77–78,
        93–94, 95
    finding out what others think and,
        128–129
    neurobiology of, 47–51, 56
    when our beliefs are challenged, 167–172
Prozac, 53
psychological skill building, 12–13, 41
    spotlight effect and, 118
    systematic desensitization and, 56–58
psychology, 121–127
    sports, 122–125
public opinion, 10, 31
purpose, 82–84, 152, 157

Raichle, Marcus, 103–104
Ramachandran, V. S., 133
raptus, 20
reciprocal inhibition, 59
Red Bull High Performance program,
    45–47
reflexes, 48–58
regrets, 179–187
Regula, Lauren, 1–3, 4, 12–13
rejection, 32–33
    avoidance of, 33–35
    responding phase and, 39–41
relationships, 31–33
    conditional self-worth and, 92–94,
        95–96
    connections and, 152–153
    culture of self and, 155–157
    disconnecting from, 41
    interconnectedness and, 159–160

interpersonal expectancy effect and, 141
    myth of self-reliance and, 158
    with others like us, 116
    our social nature and, 149–164
    romantic, 37
    the separate self and, 154
    whose opinions matter and, 173–177
resilience, 83
resources
    the brain's use of, 104–105
    conditional self-worth and, 94
    performance-based identity and, 77–78
    used by FOPO, 34–35
    wasted on attempts at control, 23–24
responding phase, 39–41
responses
    choosing how to make, 30–31
    in classical conditioning, 51–52
    to others' opinions, 173–177
    when our beliefs are challenged,
        167–172
Ressler, Kerry, 50
Rock, Brad, 64
Rodman, Dennis, 65
romantic relationships, 37
Ross, Lee, 151
roundtables, of trusted opinions, 175–176
rumination, 37, 73
Russell, Bryon, 65
Ryan, Richard, 92

Saint-Exupéry, Antoine de, 101
Samuels, Steven M., 151
scarcity, 181
Schiffman, Richard, 157
Seattle Seahawks, 8–9
selective serotonin reuptake inhibitors
    (SSRIs), 52–53
self, sense of
    culture of self and, 154–157
    interconnectedness and, 159–160
    learner's mindset and, 79–82

    poor, 41–42
    separateness and, 154–164
    strong, identity and, 78–79
    See also identity
self determination theory (SDT), 92
self-discovery, 41
self-efficacy, 74
self-esteem, 5
    social acceptance/rejection and, 32–33
self-help industry, 157
self-protection, 77–78
self-reflection, 73
self-reliance, 158
self-worth, 72–74, 87–99
    conditional, the price of, 92–95
    contingencies of, 90–92
    definition of, 89
    exercise on awareness and, 98–99
    how we learn about, 95–97
    inherent value and, 97–98
    relationships and, 92–94
Seneca, 184–185
Shackleton, Ernest, 121–122
Sherlin, Leslie, 45–47
Simon, Daniel, 139
single-point mindfulness, 108
sociability, 31–33, 149–164
    connections and, 152–153
    culture of self and, 154–157
    interconnectedness and, 159–160
    myth of self-reliance and, 158
    separate self and, 154
social anxiety disorder, 61
social context, 155–157
social intelligence, 37
social media, 137–138
social norms, 40
specialization, 71–72
Spencer, Herbert, 29
sports psychology, 122–125
spotlight effect, 113–120
    anchoring and, 116–117
    counteracting, 119–120

spotlight effect (*continued*)
definition of, 113–115
"likeness" of others and, 116
when it really is in effect, 117–118
status, social, 35
Steffel, Mary, 132, 133
steroid use, 149–150
stimulus and response, 30–31, 51–52
Stoicism, 184–185
stress
challenged beliefs and, 170
embracing, 81–82
external validation and, 91, 95
reflex response to, 49–50
success
culture of self and, 155–156
measuring, 10
in self-esteem, 89
Super Bowl, 8–9
surnames, 69–70
Sutherland, Rory, 97
Swafford, Jan, 20
sympathetic nervous system, 49, 78
systematic desensitization, 53–60

Tao Te Ching, 24
Team Canada, 1–3, 4
technology
human connection and, 154
performance-based identity and, 71–72
Thoreau, Henry David, 107
thoughts
ability to know others', 121–136
being alone with your, 101–103
negative, 105–106
See also brain
threat reflex, 49–50
time, as commodity, 181–185
Tocqueville, Alexis de, 155
trip wires, 163
trust, 175–176
Tucker, Albert, 150

Tversky, Amos, 116
Twain, Mark, 87

Umhauf, Michael, 24
US Surfing, 9
Utah Jazz, 63–66

validation, external, 29–31
performance-based identity and,
73–74
value
externalizing your sense of, 5
inherent, 97–98
performance-based identity and,
72–74
placed on others' opinions, 35
of purpose versus approval, 82–84
See also self-worth
values, 152, 180–187
core, 84–85
See also purpose
Vernadsky, Vladimir, 161
virtues, 162–164

Wallace, David Foster, 113
Ware, Bronnie, 179–180
Wason, Peter, 142
Watson, David, 60
white and gold/blue and black dress,
137–138
Williams, Ziv, 129
Wilson, Timothy, 101–102
Wolfe, Connie, 90–91
word choice, 38

Yosemite Search and Rescue, 7–8

Zoloft, 53

Acknowledgments

To Lisa, the love of my life. My heart swells at the clarity with which you share your love with me. I'm in awe of your steadfast ability to live authentically. Your unwavering commitment to our family is a blessed breeze, a gracefully timed and right-paced wind that carries our experiences with love and adventure. It's because of you that I no longer pray for calm waters, but to rather test the strength of our sails. Your love has taught me the true meaning of acceptance. I love you deeply.

To my son, Grayson, your courage, strength, and kindness inspire me every day. Your presence is a constant reminder of how to meet the moment head-on, with a twist of humor.

To my family: My mom, dad, and sister for laying the foundation of my life. Your love and guidance have provided me with a solid base and the freedom to explore. To Nana, you were my biggest champion, always. To Gramp, you lived the "think well to be well" life. To Mario, Rita, Papi, Abuela, Lori, and Doctors Mora and Beers, you've shown up over the past three decades in more ways than I have space to write about. And for that I'm forever grateful.

To Kevin Lake, your brilliant and unwavering dedication has breathed life into every page of this book. I'm incredibly grateful for your deep and honest exploration of how each concept lives inside both of us. You are a guiding torch for living the first rule of mastery. Thank you for the weight of your contribution.

To the entire Finding Mastery team, thank you for sharing my passion and purpose. Your collective expertise and grit have elevated this project beyond my wildest dreams.

To Gary DeBlasio, my mentor, thank you for being a truth mirror. Your guidance and wisdom have gracefully illuminated my invisible limits and challenged me to fundamentally work from the inside out.

To each of my clients, thank you for trusting me with your deepest dreams, insights, and fears. Your bravery inspires me and reinforces the profound impact we can have on each other's lives.

To Kevin Evers, the dedicated editor of this book and champion of clarity. You saw what this could become, and I'm grateful for how you guided the process from its inception to its current form.

Lastly, to you, the reader, thank you for trusting the guiding hand of a recommendation or the serendipitous process that led you to this book. My deepest hope is that the time we spend together adds to your life in a meaningful way. I am profoundly grateful.

About the Authors

MICHAEL GERVAIS, PHD, is one of the world's top high-performance psychologists. His clients include world record holders, Olympians, internationally acclaimed artists and musicians, MVPs from every major sport, and *Fortune* 100 CEOs. He is also the founder of Finding Mastery, a high-performance psychology consulting agency, the host of the *Finding Mastery* podcast, and the cocreator of the Performance Science Institute at the University of Southern California.

KEVIN LAKE is the Chief Creative Officer at Finding Mastery. He has collaborated with some of the world's leading performers. He produced *Gleason*, a feature documentary film that was short-listed for an Academy Award. He created and produced *Playing It Forward* in partnership with Robert Downey Jr. and Susan Downey. For seven years, he led the film division of Mel Gibson's Icon Productions.